SOFTWARE PROJECT SECRETS

WHY SOFTWARE PROJECTS FAIL

SOFTWARE PROJECT SECRETS

WHY SOFTWARE PROJECTS FAIL

George Stepanek

Apress®

Software Project Secrets: Why Software Projects Fail

ISBN 978-1-4302-5101-9

ISBN 978-1-4302-5102-6 (eBook)

President and Publisher: Paul Manning
Lead Editor: Dominic Shakeshaft
Technical Reviewer: David Putnam
Editorial Board: Steve Anglin, Mark Beckner, Ewan Buckingham, Gary Cornell, Louise Corrigan, Morgan Ertel, Jonathan Gennick, Jonathan Hassell, Robert Hutchinson, Michelle Lowman, James Markham, Matthew Moodie, Jeff Olson, Jeffrey Pepper, Douglas Pundick, Ben Renow-Clarke, Dominic Shakeshaft, Gwenan Spearing, Matt Wade, Tom Welsh
Coordinating Editor: Ellie Fountain
Copy Editor: Liz Welch
Compositor: Dina Quan
Indexer: Carol Burbo
Artist: Kinetic Publishing Services, LLC
Cover Designer: Anna Ishchenko

Distributed to the book trade worldwide by Springer Science+Business Media New York, 233 Spring Street, 6th Floor, New York, NY 10013. Phone 1-800-SPRINGER, fax (201) 348-4505, e-mail orders-ny@springer-sbm.com, or visit www.springeronline.com. Apress Media, LLC is a California LLC and the sole member (owner) is Springer Science + Business Media Finance Inc (SSBM Finance Inc). SSBM Finance Inc is a Delaware corporation.

For information on translations, please e-mail rights@apress.com, or visit www.apress.com.

Apress and friends of ED books may be purchased in bulk for academic, corporate, or promotional use. eBook versions and licenses are also available for most titles. For more information, reference our Special Bulk Sales–eBook Licensing web page at www.apress.com/bulk-sales.

To Erica, without whom I would not be who I am today

Contents at a Glance

Contents

PART I
WHY SOFTWARE PROJECTS FAIL . . .

PART II
. . . AND HOW TO MAKE THEM SUCCEED

About the Author

An experienced team leader and software developer, George Stepanek has gained certification as an architect in J2EE (Java 2 Enterprise Edition) and as an MCSD (Microsoft Certified Solution Developer) in .NET. Born in the Czech Republic, he grew up in England and later emigrated to New Zealand. He studied natural science and philosophy at the University of Cambridge—achieving an MA—followed by postgraduate diplomas in computer science and education. He has worked for a range of IT companies, most recently at Unisys New Zealand. He is passionate about creating quality software and sharing new and interesting ideas. His interest in education has taken him to Wikipedia (the free encyclopedia), where his writing has achieved featured article status.

About the Technical Reviewer

Previously a mentor at Exoftware, where his role took him to a variety of organizations, David Putnam has acted as an advisor on the management of software development projects to companies in three continents. Now the manager of CentaurNet, part of Centaur Publishing, David still regularly presents papers, workshops, and tutorials on the management and practice of software development at national and international events, including XP2002, XP2003, XP2004, and XP2005. Until recently he wrote the "Models and Methodologies" column for *Application Development Advisor* magazine and has had articles published in other publications. His main interests are people management, software development, and learning organizations, and making work satisfying to all those involved.

About the Technical Reviewer

Acknowledgments

The following people deserve their share of the credit:

Richard Cheeseman,
Andrew Chessum,
Kimson Co,
Alistair Cockburn,
Greg Forsythe,
Dave Horton,
Jasmine Kamante,
Eugene Sergejew,
Dominic Shakeshaft,
Olga Stepanek, and,
of course,
my sweet Erica.

To them my thanks are due for suggestions, advice, inspiration, encouragement, expert opinions, and other such things. Without their help, this book wouldn't have been half as good.

Special thanks go to Unisys for their support during the writing of this book, to the whole Apress team for their patience and their hard work, and to Emily Cotlier for improving my writing with a wealth of advice and editing input.

George Stepanek

WHY SOFTWARE PROJECTS FAIL ...

Introduction

Your boss has asked you to oversee the development of a new billing system, and you've brought together a capable project manager and a group of hand-picked developers. They've chosen state-of-the-art technologies and tools to build the system. The business analyst has talked at length with the accounting manager, and has written up a detailed set of requirements. The project has everything it needs to be a success—doesn't it?

Apparently not. Six months later the project is already late and over budget. The developers have been working overtime for weeks, and one has already quit, but despite this the software never seems to get any closer to completion. Part of the problem is that the accounting team keeps claiming that the software doesn't do what they need, and they have pushed through a steady stream of "essential" change requests, not to mention a flood of bug reports. Your boss will be furious when she hears about this.

So what went wrong?

Whatever it is, it must be something that most companies get wrong. According to Standish Group [2001] research, only 28 percent of software projects in 2000 succeeded outright (see Figure 1-1). Some 23 percent were canceled, and the remainder were substantially late (by 63 percent on average), over budget (by 45 percent), lacking features (by 33 percent), or, very often, all of those issues combined.

At New Zealand's Ministry of Justice, the new $42 million Case Management System was $8 million over budget and over a year late when it was rolled out in 2003. Of the 27 benefits expected from the system, only 16 have been realized. Instead of boosting productivity, the system has actually increased the time needed to manage court cases by doubling the amount of data entry. A postimplementation review identified over 1,400 outstanding issues. But "the only challenges faced by the developers were those common to large and complex systems" [Bell 2004].

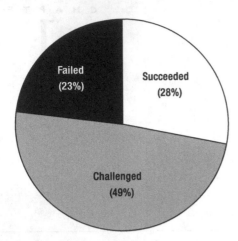

Figure 1-1. The success and failure of software projects in 2000

In contrast, things look very different in the engineering and construction industry. According to the *Engineering News-Record*, 94 percent of the project customers they queried were satisfied with the results of their projects, which suggests that construction projects have much lower failure rates than software projects. That's why the collapse of the tube-shaped roof in the newly constructed terminal 2E at Charles de Gaulle airport (Paris) in May 2004 made front-page news around the world: it was so unusual. Failed software projects are far too common to merit such attention.

We can learn why by looking at commercial and noncommercial software development. Commercial software is produced by companies for profit. Some software is custom written for individual clients, such as your billing system, but there are also generic "off-the-shelf" products like Microsoft Word. Virtually all of these are created within a project, or within a series of projects.

Noncommercial software is very often *open source*, which means that anyone can read its source code. Users can find out how it works, and make changes to fix bugs and add the features they want. With open source software, developers from around the world work together on software that has no fixed feature list, budget, or deadline. Open source developers coordinate their efforts in ways that are quite different from traditional project management.

Open source software is a huge success. "The Internet runs on open source software (BIND, Sendmail, Apache, Perl)," says Tim O'Reilly, CEO of O'Reilly & Associates, one of the largest publishers of computer books. Open source software generally has far fewer reliability issues or bugs than commercial software. But is it a success by the same criteria we use to measure commercial projects? After all, with unlimited time, wouldn't every project succeed?

It's true that unlimited time can compensate for poor productivity. However, the productivity of open source developers is legendary. In 1991 Linus Torvalds wrote a complete, stable, operating system kernel (Linux) in less than a year, substantially on his own at that stage. And less than a year after eight core contributors came together to form the Apache Group, they had made Apache 1.0 so compelling a piece of software that it became the most widely used webpage server on the Internet.

These successes suggest that software development can work very well outside traditional project management. This is perplexing, considering that project management techniques work well in most other areas. We have seen that this is true for construction and engineering. There must be something quite different about software development that makes project management fail.

The next chapter will begin the analysis by identifying the characteristics of software, and of the software development process, that make them unique. These characteristics will then be compared against project management's best practices to discover where the process of project management breaks down for software development. The first part of the book closes with a simulated case study that shows how these problems can cause an otherwise promising project to fail.

These chapters describe the problems in software development in some detail. This may seem discouraging, but don't abandon hope just yet. Identifying the source of a problem is the first step toward finding a solution.

The second part of the book focuses on strategies that can help to bring software projects to a successful conclusion. It begins by surveying three popular and promising new software development methodologies. It then considers ways to reconcile these methodologies with project management. Finally, the case study from Part One is reworked to show how the same project could have succeeded by using the new techniques.

Why Software Is Different

When we try to find out what's different about software and software development, the first question that comes to mind is "Different from what?" So let's compare software development to road building. We've all used roads; we know what they're for and how they work. Roads are a very different product from software. In their massive and immobile simplicity, they're as unlike software as it is possible to be.

There are many differences between road building and software development. Software development is rarely affected by the weather, for example, whereas you shouldn't begin excavating a cutting if the slope is soaking wet and subject to landslip. But is this a fundamental difference? No. Software projects are also affected by external events. If a third-party software component isn't available on time, for example, then similar delays can occur.

The following sections introduce 12 distinct but interrelated differences between software development and other common business endeavors (see Figure 2-1). Road building has been chosen as the example to compare against because it displays none of these characteristics, so distinctions can be drawn as clearly as possible. However, this may not be the case for any other activities that come to mind, which might exhibit one or two, or even a few of these characteristics. What makes software development unique is that it encompasses them all.

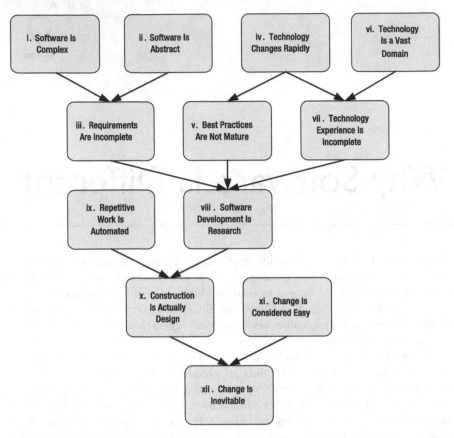

Figure 2-1. The 12 sections in this chapter each introduce one characteristic that is unique to software development, and explain its relationship to those already discussed. The concepts that appear further down on the diagram are derived from the more basic concepts shown at the top.

1. Software Is Complex

"The drive to reduce complexity is at the heart of software development" [McConnell 2004]. Even minor software can accumulate frightening complexity. A small program with one or two authors can easily run into tens of thousands of lines of code. Significant products, like the latest versions of Microsoft Windows, run into tens of millions. But numbers of lines of code may not mean much to you until you can relate that measurement to other types of complex systems.

When you look at software as it's being written, it appears as a sequence of *instructions*. Instructions usually appear as a single line in the text, but very complex instructions sometimes span two or more lines. An instruction may copy a piece of data, perform some arithmetic, manipulate text, or decide which parts of the program to execute (and in what order). There are also blank lines to separate groups of instructions, comments that explain to other programmers what these instructions are intended to accomplish, and elements that help define the structure of the program (*components*, *objects*, *methods*, etc.—please see the Glossary for more details).

But the most important part of the code is the instructions. You can think of an instruction as being equivalent to a moving part in a vehicle. An instruction, just like a moving part, takes a varying input and does something with it.

You might expect that a 100,000-line program would be ten times more complex than a 10,000-line program. However, a program's complexity depends not just on the instructions, but also on the interactions between the instructions. The 100,000-line program has ten times as many instructions interacting with ten times as many instructions, so we should actually expect it to be a hundred times as complex.

Skilled developers endeavor to reduce this overall level of complexity by isolating various parts of system from each other. These are sectioned off into small pieces (called objects) or somewhat larger pieces (called components), which are chunks of code that can be used without knowing exactly how they work. They hide the complexity of their internal mechanisms behind simple interfaces. This technique is known as *encapsulation*, and it is a key part of *object-oriented programming*.

Figure 2-2 shows how it works. This system is composed of 12 items (of some kind) that interact with each other. By dividing these items into four smaller assemblages, the total number of interactions has been reduced from 66 to 18, and the system is now much less complex.

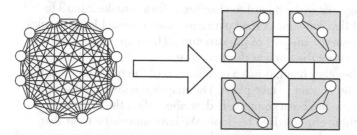

Figure 2-2. Simplifying a complex system by dividing it into smaller pieces

Despite such techniques, developers still find that the complexity of their software increases faster than its size.

Computer programs are the most intricate, delicately balanced and finely interwoven of all the products of human industry to date. They are machines with far more moving parts than any engine: the parts don't wear out, but they interact and rub up against one another in ways the programmers themselves cannot predict. [Gleik 1992]

NOTE Software is unique in that its most significant issue is its complexity.

2. Software Is Abstract

You can't physically touch software. You can hold a floppy disk or CD-ROM in your hand, but the software itself is a ghost that can be moved from one object to another with little difficulty. In contrast, a road is a solid object that has a definite size and shape. You can touch the material and walk the route. Even the foundations, which are hidden when the road is completed, can be viewed and touched as the road is being built.

Software is a codification of a huge set of behaviors: if this occurs, then that should happen, and so on. We can visualize individual behaviors, but we have great difficulty visualizing large numbers of sequential and alternative behaviors.

That's why playing chess well is so difficult. At its simplest level, chess is just a game where 32 pieces move from square to square across a board. We can think of each move as a piece's behavior, but any single move is meaningless in isolation. What gives it significance is its relationship to the moves that have gone before, and to the moves that are yet to come. These relationships are entirely abstract. It's a huge task to accurately assess them, and by doing so draw up a sound strategy. That's why there's such a gulf between novice and expert chess players.

The same things that make it hard to visualize software make it hard to draw blueprints of that software. A road plan can show the exact location, elevation, and dimensions of any part of the structure. The map corresponds to the structure, but it's not the same as the structure.

Software, on the other hand, is just a codification of the behaviors that the programmers and users want to take place. The map is the same as the structure. Once the system has been completely described, then the software has been created. Nothing else needs to be done. We have automatic tools that convert this representation into a program that the computer can execute.

This means that software can only ever be described accurately at the level of individual instructions. To summarize is to remove essential details, and such details can (as we've all experienced) cause the software to fail catastrophically or—worse—subtly and insidiously. But no one can hold 10,000 or 100,000 operations in mind at once.

Even encapsulation, which can reduce the overall complexity of a system, doesn't release us from the burden of having to individually define each and every one of these instructions (or behaviors); it just helps us to organize them better.

A map or a blueprint for a piece of software must greatly simplify the representation in order to be comprehensible. But by doing so, it becomes inaccurate and ultimately incorrect. This is an important realization: any architecture, design, or diagram we create for software is essentially inadequate. If we represent every detail, then we're merely duplicating the software in another form, and we're wasting our time and effort.

NOTE Software is the most abstract product that can be created in a project.

3. Requirements Are Incomplete

Software is normally commissioned for the needs of users and managers, not professional developers. These individuals are experts in their own roles, but they rarely have as much experience as professional developers in dealing with the abstraction and complexity of software. They understand the business processes much better than the developers, of course, but even when someone has a good grasp of the main flows of behavior that are required, it's still very difficult to take into account all of the alternative flows and error conditions, and how different sets of requirements relate to each other.

Moreover, as we saw in the previous section, it is impossible to accurately blueprint software, or draw up a complete set of requirements before the software has been completed in some form or another. This means that any specification of requirements for software is likely to be incomplete in important ways.

The users will gain new insights into their needs as the software starts to take shape. The software becomes less abstract to them once they can get hands-on experience and try out a variety of scenarios. This is where the "steady stream of 'essential' change requests" for the billing system comes from. It's not that users don't know what they want: it's that they're just not able to visualize a system of this complexity until it's at least partially complete.

To be successful, users and developers must work together to refine the requirements for the software. As the software grows in functionality, the users can revise the remaining features based on their testing of the system under construction. An expert can be brought in at any stage to perform usability testing, and to make recommendations regarding the user interface.

All of this suggests that the belief that you have, or ever can have, a comprehensive and finalized set of requirements is a self-deception. The most honest response that a user can give is "I'll know what I want when I see it." However, as we'll see later, this consideration is rarely taken into account.

Does this matter? The Standish Group [2001] identified problems with requirements and specifications as the top "Project Challenged Factors" for software projects. They were the most significant issues for 42 percent of projects.

In contrast, drawing up the specifications for a new road is a relatively straightforward process: only the route, number of lanes, intersections, surfacing, and so on need to be defined. Any driver can understand and recognize the value of these characteristics.

NOTE It is uniquely difficult to define a complete set of requirements for software before beginning development.

4. Technology Changes Rapidly

Twenty years ago we were struggling with the MS-DOS operating system and creating simple spreadsheets on our PCs. Today we edit video on our computers and connect to systems across the world. Computers double in speed about every two years, and this opens up more and more opportunities for software developers. Software changes quickly—we all know that—but we may not be aware of just how quickly it changes, and what impact this has on any new software we try to build.

Nowadays any significant new software is almost certain to be built with an *enterprise application framework* such as Sun Microsystems' Java 2 Enterprise Edition (J2EE) or Microsoft .NET. It's important to understand just what this phrase means, because these technologies largely define the software development landscape as it stands today:

- A framework is a toolkit, just like a Lego set, that you can use to build a variety of items. In the case of software, the building blocks are bits of software that do jobs that have been found useful in a wide range of situations. Examples include getting data from a database, drawing a window on the screen, or converting dates from one format to another.

- The word "application" includes more than you might imagine. There are the one-person desktop applications that we're all familiar with, such as Microsoft Word for word processing, but there are also multiuser applications that run on an office network, such as accounting and email. Beyond that are applications we use over the Internet, such as Amazon.com's online ordering and Google's search page, and applications that other applications use to exchange information, so that international phone calls can get connected, for example.

- "Enterprise" is the most difficult word to define. Perhaps the best way to think of it is "as big as you want." Desktop applications are limited to running on one computer, but that's OK because only one person is using them at a time. The popular Internet search engine Google provides information to more than 1,000 people every second: no single computer could handle that load. Enterprise technology allows many computers to work together for a single application, and also provides the connectivity to allow lots of people to access it at the same time. But "enterprise" also means "as small as you want": enterprise application frameworks are not just for major applications in big companies.

Given that some of the most important government and business software is now being built with these enterprise application frameworks, you might expect that they have a long and distinguished history, and that they'd be stable and mature products. That's not the case. Sun's J2EE, which was perhaps the first true enterprise application framework to be widely used, appeared in 1998, and has seen considerable change since then. Microsoft only released its competing technology (.NET) in 2002, and no one has more than a couple of years of experience with it yet.

In contrast, we've been building roads for thousands of years, ever since the time of the ancient Roman and Chinese civilizations. The problem is well understood, and the technologies change slowly. Hot-mix asphalt was patented in 1903, and that basic technology is still what we use today.

NOTE Software development technologies change faster than other construction technologies.

5. Best Practices Are Not Mature

Technologies can be used skillfully or unskillfully. For software, this distinction can often only be assessed some time after the software has been completed. The presence or lack of software quality shows up most clearly in its *extensibility*.

> *Extensibility is the ability to add functionality or modify existing functionality without impacting existing system functionality. You cannot measure extensibility when the system is deployed, but it shows up the first time you must extend the functionality of the system.*
> *[Cade and Roberts 2002]*

Most programmers have had the painful experience of trying to modify a system that works well, but in which it's virtually impossible to make changes without breaking some of its functionality. Programmers call this *fragile code*.

Fragile code can have a big financial impact. Numerous studies have shown that at least 50 percent of software cost goes into extending and modifying the original system [Koskinen 2004], and modifications to fragile code can be twice as expensive as modifications to robust and flexible code. Clients need solutions that can change and grow along with them.

Code becomes fragile when it's put together in an ad hoc fashion, without sufficient attention being paid to its architecture. An architecture is the overall structure and design of a system, and can be seen as a codification of how to use the technologies that the system is built upon. New technologies need new architectures. For example, when Microsoft introduced "event-driven programming" to BASIC in 1991 via its new Visual Basic development environment, it provided powerful new capabilities, but also the potential for new problems.

One of these problems was a poor design practice, which became so prevalent that it ended up with a name of its own: the Magic Pushbutton. In event-driven programming, all a programmer does is write a few "event handlers," which are routines that respond to the user's actions. This technology means that instead of having to write the core functionality for each new program over and over again, a programmer can just add functionality to an application skeleton that's provided for them.

In the Magic Pushbutton, the only event handler that does any real work is the one that's called when the user clicks the OK button. If the programmer doesn't deliberately organize the program's code in a better way, then it all accumulates in this one routine, which ends up as a huge, unmanageable blob of code.

Over time, every field of human endeavor develops best practices to counter common mistakes like this. A best practice is a process or technique that has a proven record of success in providing significant improvement to the results of an activity. Experience allows users to define the best practices—in other words, the most consistent ways to use the technology well.

But how long should we wait for those best practices? Object-oriented programming has been in use since 1980, but it was only in 1995 that the "Gang of Four" (Erich Gamma, Richard Helm, Ralph Johnson, and John Vlissides) published their seminal book *Design Patterns*, which revolutionized object-oriented architectures and provided solutions to "anti-patterns" such as the Magic Pushbutton. Fifteen years is a long time in the IT industry: many technologies have come and gone in less time.

The enterprise application frameworks we've discussed have been around for only a fraction of that time. A few architecture books are available already, but none of them are as significant as *Design Patterns*. This suggests that the enterprise application frameworks' best practices aren't mature yet.

So is software based on new technologies necessarily poor? Fortunately, no. Later sections in this chapter will show how robust software can be created even in these circumstances, but it's not as simple as in road building, where the basic technologies have been around for much longer, and hence the best practices are long established and almost universally applied.

NOTE Most software development technologies are not mature enough to have a set of proven best practices.

6. Technology Is a Vast Domain

"No man is an island, entire of itself." Nor does any piece of software exist in isolation. We've seen how the building blocks for any new software would come from an enterprise application framework, and they would implement the most commonly used tasks that the software performs. These tasks are many and varied, and it comes as no surprise that the enterprise application frameworks themselves are huge and complex, containing tens of thousands of usable routines. You can think of each routine as a knob, button, or dial that allows the application—and the developer—to control the workings of the framework, although there are also some routines that behave more like stand-alone tools.

However challenging it is to develop software using an enterprise application framework, it's still much simpler and quicker than attempting to create your own versions of these tools from scratch. It's always cheaper to buy than to build, which is why a substantial marketplace has sprung up for software components that are more specialized than those available in the enterprise application frameworks.

Until recently, these software components were distributed on CD-ROMs, and copied into any application that required them. Since then, *web services* have become the preferred technology for accessing third-party software components. For all the hype surrounding web services, they are in principle very simple. Instead of selling CD-ROMs, a third party keeps their software components on their own servers and makes them available over the Internet for a fee. This makes it easy for the vendor to apply bug fixes and enhancements, and enables them to provide access to interesting data (stock quotes, news, retail price comparisons, etc.) as well as useful tools.

Enterprise application frameworks contain a wealth of functionality, and beyond that there is even more functionality available from third-party software components. A single application would use only a few of these routines and components. Even when working on a variety of applications and systems, a developer will not be able to gain experience with more than a small proportion of the technologies that are available.

NOTE Software development has far more technologies, and its technologies have far more complexity than a single individual can hope to gain expertise with.

7. Technology Experience Is Incomplete

We've already seen that software technologies change rapidly. New technologies supplant older ones every few years, and even more frequently, new versions of existing technology appear that radically change the functionality and use of that technology. This change is necessary and inevitable.

For example, Microsoft's BizTalk Server 2004 is a very different product from BizTalk Server 2000. Some of the tools work like they did in the previous version, but the majority are entirely new or have changed beyond recognition. "The core purpose of BizTalk Server remains, but Microsoft has redesigned or enhanced almost everything around that core" [Yager 2004].

Moreover, developers work with an enormous range of specialized third-party software components. Experience with these components can rarely be carried over into future projects, because those future projects are unlikely to use the same third-party components. Experience with enterprise application frameworks is similar; these frameworks are so extensive that different projects that use the same framework may well use totally different parts of it.

Whatever a developer was working on even three to four years ago is unlikely to be of any direct use today. So what use is an experienced developer? Is it true that every significant new piece of software is written by developers who are essentially novices to the task?

It's true that long lists of desired technology skills, which are so prevalent in IT job advertisements, are virtually useless. The bulk of the technical knowledge required for a project will normally be learned on the job. However, the "softer" skills that make one a good developer, or even a good team leader or architect, do apply from one project to the next, and can accumulate over time. These skills include the software development best practices that are discussed later in this book. Sadly, these skills are rarely mentioned in job ads. They're harder to assess: you can't just boil them down to a list of buzzwords and acronyms.

> **NOTE** Expertise with particular software development technologies is very quickly outdated, and therefore most specific skills are learned on the job.

8. Software Development Is Research

As noted in previous points, the requirements for a piece of software will invariably be incomplete. There will be conceptual gaps that must be filled, and there will be assumptions that aren't justified and aspects that just won't work. Because clients aren't software experts, they won't always be able to distinguish between what's possible and what's not, or know what trade-offs are available. They need to work with the developers to discover this.

This means that the development process is a process of discovery—progressively finding out the exact character of the software that will meet the customer's needs. Developers must combine analytical and creative skills to find out what their customer really wants (even if the customer's description is confused and incomplete) and invent ways to combine these requirements into a system that's logically consistent and easy to use.

The project will probably include software tools and components that are new or unfamiliar to the developers. New technology doesn't always match up to the marketing claims that are made for it. The rate of change in technology has been accelerating, and products are often released before they're mature, complete, or bug-free. The advantages of being first to the market can outweigh the drawbacks of proffering flawed software.

For these reasons, users need to be wary of "version 1.0" software: software that has just been released for the first time. Many companies "get it right" only on the second or third attempt. Just think about Windows 3.1 and Internet Explorer 3.0: who remembers any of their earlier versions?

These issues are particularly relevant for beta software. Traditionally, after in-house testing is completed, new software would be given to a small group of carefully chosen customers for *beta testing* in real-world conditions. This would uncover yet more bugs, which were fixed before the first general release. Recently, however, some software publishers have begun selling beta releases to their customers. This means that the first released version is known to contain bugs, and that customers are expected to pay for the privilege of testing it and finding the bugs. Other publishers do the same, but don't even mention that the software is beta.

We can't take it for granted that a given software tool or component will work as we expect it to, or do everything that we need when we use it to create our software. Even if the product chosen is mature and well regarded, and even if the developers have used it before, because of the complexity of software, you can rarely be sure that it can be used for the functions and circumstances that are unique to a particular project. You can't tell if it will do the job until you've actually made it do the job, and have seen that it works.

So software development is also a process of discovering whether and how the chosen technology can be made to perform the role that's required of it. Sometimes it will work as expected. Sometimes it won't, but there's a workaround that takes more effort than originally planned. And sometimes the technology just can't do what's needed. Software projects rarely run smoothly from beginning to end. They frequently encounter setbacks and dead ends, simply because of the scope of the unknown. In a very real sense software projects are simply the process of discovering the unknowns: once the unknowns are known, then the project is effectively at an end.

NOTE Software development isn't just a process of creating software; it's also a process of learning how to create the software that is best suited for its purpose.

9. Repetitive Work Is Automated

Automation is the automatic operation and control of a piece of equipment, or of an entire system. The use of automation began during the Industrial Revolution in the eighteenth century, and hasn't let up any time since then. We expect productivity gains in every industry, and software and road building are no exceptions.

In some industries, manufacturing is done in factories that are empty of workers except for a few maintenance staff, and production has been completely automated. But we're discussing projects here rather than production, and projects can never be wholly automated. The Project Management Institute [2000] defines a project as "a temporary endeavor undertaken to create a unique product or service." It's this uniqueness that makes complete automation impossible. No road is just like another, and even a piece of software that duplicates the behavior of another must be made in a unique way. This is called a "clean room" implementation.

No matter how much labor is saved through the use of machinery in road making, road workers must still do a substantial amount of repetitive work. Asphalt must be laid and rolled. Median barriers and lane markings must be installed.

All of the repetitive work can be automated in software development, and that's because software doesn't exist in the real world. It resides in the controlled environment of the computer. Every part of it can be created and controlled by means of a wide range of software tools.

Common tasks and services are included in enterprise application frameworks, and more specialized ones can be done by third-party software components, so programmers work more efficiently because much of their work has already been done for them. But even beyond that, tools are constantly being developed and refined to automate new chores and responsibilities.

One example is in web services. Web services use the industry-standard messaging language Extensible Markup Language (XML) to communicate messages over the Internet. To create a web service, you must define the message format for every possible type of message, to show how the data is to be converted into XML. This is a labor-intensive chore. But not long after the introduction of web services, Microsoft automated this step in its Visual Studio .NET development environment. Developers no longer have to put any effort into defining the XML message formats for their web services, because this work is now done for them by their development tools.

NOTE Software development has been automated to a greater degree than other project-based activities.

10. Construction Is Actually Design

Road building consists of a sequence of well-defined phases. The first step is to perform the planning and design, which results in a set of plans and blueprints that can be signed off. Once these tasks are completed, then construction can start. The construction phase largely consists of well-defined, repetitive tasks that can be accomplished by less highly skilled workers.

In contrast, software development is a process of research, so at no point can definitive plans be drawn up. The more definitive you try to make the plans, the more flawed they'll be, and the more labor there will be in revising them to meet changing circumstances. As the shape of the software becomes increasingly clear over the course of a project, the design of that software must be revised again and again. To completely redesign the solution each time around would be onerous and wasteful, so we should think rather of a process of ongoing design.

We've seen that the repetitive work in software development is rapidly automated. There aren't any repetitive tasks to define. But if tasks aren't repetitive, then defining them exhaustively becomes a time-consuming process. And there is little to be gained from defining tasks in this way. Software is abstract, so defining the construction tasks completely is equivalent to actually performing the work, because automated tools are available that can turn such designs into working software.

If tasks can't be well defined, then we can't cleanly separate the design and construction phases. Indeed, there's no construction as such; there's only design on smaller and smaller scales. This means that we can't easily categorize people into the roles of architect, designer, programmer, or analyst. The roles overlap. All developers have the same kinds of tasks to perform, even though some may have more responsibilities than others.

When a developer creates a new feature in a piece of software, their task is simply to answer the question "exactly how is this feature going to work?" They will add a set of instructions to the source code that defines in every detail how the feature will work. But each detail is a design choice. For example, a piece of text can be stored in an unchangeable object for greater efficiency, or in a changeable object for greater flexibility. Which option is chosen depends on how that piece of text is used. It's a significant decision.

Programming is more than just writing code. Each step requires the developer to analyze some portion of the problem and design some aspect of the solution.

NOTE Unlike other products, software is not constructed, but rather designed into existence.

11. Change Is Considered Easy

Last-minute changes to requirements are rare in road building because the consequences are so severe. If you discover during the course of a project that the foundations are in the wrong place, then it takes considerable effort to dig them out and rebuild them in another place. This is obvious to clients and contractors alike.

Once you've built a section of road, then it's built. A road may be extended or widened, but it is never moved. When a road is "realigned," what happens is that a completely new section of road is built alongside the old, which often remains as an alternative route. A freeway interchange may be reworked over several years to suit changing traffic patterns by the addition of permanent bridges, ramps, and lanes in a series of projects.

This isn't to say that changes never occur in civil engineering projects. When you start digging, you may find that subsurface conditions are different from the original analysis. Subcontractors might not be available when you want them, and schedules may be adjusted accordingly. However, such changes rarely have an impact on the nature of the product: we don't expect to end up with a different building or a different road.

Compare this to software. Software is soft, by definition. Any part of it can be changed at any time, just by rewriting that portion of the code. We expect that bugs can and will be fixed wherever they appear in the system, as indeed they are. Anyone who has written macros for Microsoft Office, or learned how to write small programs at school or at a university, knows how flexible software is and how quickly you can make substantial changes.

It's true that substantial changes can often be made quickly and easily, but to properly implement them you really have to revise the architecture of the software so that it gracefully supports the new functionality; otherwise you'll just create a mess and make the software more fragile.

The architecture must be flexible and designed to accommodate change. This is the main yardstick that we have for an architecture. If the software will never be changed, then why should we care if the software is fragile and badly designed as long as it still works? But most major systems are intended for long use—often decades—even if their underlying technologies rapidly become obsolete. Over such long periods of time, the business environments will almost always see significant change.

In addition to designing the architecture, we must also design our development process to support change. This subject will be covered in much greater detail in later chapters.

NOTE Software can be modified rapidly, and this pace is expected, but it's better to implement the changes properly.

12. Change Is Inevitable

Are there any situations where there will never be changes to the software? We've seen how software development is actually a process of design from beginning to end. It includes design work to accommodate requirements whose details become clearer as the project progresses, and design work to reflect what's learned about the tools and components used to develop the software. The process of software development is one of continuous design, and therefore of continuous change.

Moreover, clients see how easily changes can be made, and expect that they can change their minds at any point. Indeed, they often do, as they learn more about what their nascent software can achieve for them. In 8,000 large software projects analyzed in one study, some 40 percent of their requirements arrived after development had begun [Jones 1995].

Change is inevitable, and if a piece of software isn't built to support change then it will fall apart even as it is being built. The quality of software shows itself when the software is first extended or modified. If the process of development becomes one of extension and modification, then any software that resists change will have a difficult gestation. Poor changes are more likely to generate defects or bugs, and will make the code fragile and hard to debug.

It's easy to see the problems that change can bring to a project, and begin to see change as the "enemy," but is attempting to eliminate all change a viable option? Once we see change as inevitable, then the issue isn't one of avoiding change but of making change work to our advantage. This is a much more manageable problem, as we'll see later.

NOTE No software is perfect as first envisioned; it will always require changes to make it best suit its role.

Summary

In this chapter we've taken a whirlwind tour of the software development landscape to set the scene for the rest of the book. We've identified 12 key characteristics of software development that make it unique. The next chapter will use these concepts as a starting point. We'll be performing an in-depth analysis of project management to discover which kinds of activities it is suited to (and which it is not), and we'll be comparing this picture to the view of software development that we developed in this chapter:

1. Software is unique in that its most significant issue is its complexity.

2. Software is the most abstract product that can be created in a project.

3. It is uniquely difficult to define a complete set of requirements for software before beginning development.

4. Software development technologies change faster than other construction technologies.

5. Most software development technologies are not mature enough to have a set of proven best practices.

6. Software development has far more technologies, and its technologies have far more complexity than a single individual can hope to gain expertise with.

7. Expertise with particular software development technologies is very quickly outdated, and therefore most specific skills are learned on the job.

8. Software development isn't just a process of creating software; it's also a process of learning how to create the software that is best suited for its purpose.

9. Software development has been automated to a greater degree than other project-based activities.

10. Unlike other products, software is not constructed, but rather designed into existence.

11. Software can be modified rapidly, and this pace is expected, but it's better to implement the changes properly.

12. No software is perfect as first envisioned; it will always require changes to make it best suit its role.

3

Project Management Assumptions

In analyzing the interactions between software development and project management, we've already examined some of the unique characteristics of software development. The next step is to analyze the corresponding features of project management in similar detail. This chapter will cover the five most relevant topics within project management, stepping through each one in turn:

- Scope management
- Time management
- Cost management
- Quality management
- Risk management

We're interested in the differences between software development projects and other types of projects, so we won't be looking at areas of project management where the differences are less significant. The following topics will therefore not be covered because they are peripheral to our analysis:

- Integration management
- Human resource management
- Communications management
- Procurement management

Hidden Assumptions

*The conventional wisdom in project management values managing
scope, cost and schedule to the original plan. . . . This mental model is
so entrenched in project management thinking that its underlying
assumptions are rarely questioned. [Poppendieck 2003]*

In this chapter we'll be looking for assumptions that aren't valid in the context
of software development projects, because they may be the fundamental reasons why software projects so often fail. We'll therefore be comparing any
assumptions we find to the 12 key characteristics of software development
that we identified in Chapter 2.

Projects can fail for other reasons, of course. Poor staff, difficult clients,
and ineffective management can all contribute to project failure. But these
factors aren't specific to software development, and they don't explain why
software development projects are particularly challenged. We want to discover why a software project might fail even in the most favorable circumstances: where there's a skilled and motivated team, and where the client has
realistic expectations.

This analysis applies just as much to projects undertaken for internal customers and clients. Software projects undertaken by a company's own developers are no more likely to succeed or fail than those done by external contractors.
The only factor that may be significantly different is that projects for external
customers always require contracts: either ongoing outsource agreements or
per-project contracts. (The issues that are specific to software project contracts
will be noted.)

Experienced project managers know when to bend and when to break the
rules. Many software projects are capably handled, and many achieve acceptable results. But trial and error is a painful way to learn. We already know
what's unique about software, so let's bear that in mind as we look over the
discipline of project management, and find the changes that must be made
if our software projects are to succeed.

The PMBOK

We'll be using the Project Management Institute's *Project Management Body
of Knowledge (PMBOK)* as a reference to describe how project management is
supposed to work. The PMBOK has been published in a number of versions
since 1987, and has since become an American National Standards Institute
(ANSI) standard. Its purpose is to identify good practices and define a common terminology for project management. The PMBOK breaks down project
management into the nine topics (or "knowledge areas") listed in the introduction to this chapter.

At the time of writing, the third edition [PMI 2004] of the PMBOK Guide has yet to be formally released, and it will doubtless take several years before its advances are widely known and used throughout the profession, so our analysis will focus on the second edition [PMI 2000]. Significant differences between this edition and the exposure draft of the third edition will be noted.

The comments here aren't a criticism of the PMBOK or of project management in general. The PMBOK describes a core project management methodology that has been successfully applied to a wide range of projects in many different industries. Because it's intended to be used in such a variety of situations, it's reasonable that it should be adjusted for a specific situation such as software development.

Scope Management

Scope definition is the process of breaking down the overall aims (or requirements) of a project into a number of smaller, more closely defined goals. These are documented in the Work Breakdown Structure, which is a diagram that represents the hierarchy of goals (Example 3-1). Each goal on one level is broken down into a number of subgoals on the next, and so on. Detailed descriptions of these goals are collected into a Work Breakdown Structure dictionary. The Work Breakdown Structure is used to produce cost and duration estimates.

Example 3-1. Part of a Sample Work Breakdown Structure for a Project to Build a New Road

```
Pedestrian crossing
    Road markings
    Traffic light
        Traffic light posts
        Electricity cables
        Controller
Bridge
    Foundations
    Pillars
    Road bed
Roundabout (etc.)
```

ASSUMPTION Scope can be completely defined.

"Is each item clearly and completely defined?" asks the PMBOK [PMI 2000]. We can see one hidden assumption already. What happens if the scope can't be completely defined? After all, in software development there's no such thing as a complete and final set of requirements. (This is one of the key characteristics of software development: the third one—"characteristic #3"—from the 12 we identified in the previous chapter.) Is it still worthwhile working toward a comprehensive scope definition, even if we can never quite get there? Or would we just be writing up meaningless details?

This is an important question because, according to the PMBOK, the next step is to obtain formal acceptance for the scope document. Often the scope definition becomes part of the contract for the project. In the event of a dispute there can be financial penalties or litigation, so we have every motivation to ensure that the process doesn't go astray.

The PMBOK [PMI 2000] gives this rationale for performing the scope definition process: "Proper scope definition is critical to project success. 'When there is poor scope definition, final project costs can be expected to be higher because of the inevitable changes which disrupt project rhythm, cause rework, increase project time, and lower the productivity and morale of the workforce.'"

According to the PMBOK, a poor scope definition is one that's incomplete or inaccurate. But software is extraordinarily complex, so a scope definition for software development would include a considerable amount of detail. The implication is that the more detail there is, the better, at least if it helps to define the various items more precisely.

It's easy to be lulled into a false sense of security by having a very detailed scope definition. For software, since the requirements are always incomplete (characteristic #3), the more detail there is in a requirements definition, the more inaccurate it becomes. The critical question is: would it be better to include details that are known to be at least partially wrong, or would it be better to initially omit this level of detail?

In practice, inaccuracies will always result in rework. Unless the client just doesn't care, or has given up in despair, they'll always insist on making changes to the software to ensure that it behaves in the way they think it should. That they initially didn't quite know, or couldn't quite describe how the software should work, isn't their fault. They're not the experts.

Omissions may result in rework, but only if the developers make assumptions about missing details as they develop the software. If they can consult with the client whenever some details need to be elaborated, then there will be little or no rework. We can think of this as "just-in-time" requirements gathering.

An overly detailed scope definition will therefore result in more changes, not fewer.

The PMBOK asks us to tightly lock down the project's scope before starting work on the project. Changes are shown in a bad light, and only the negative consequences are discussed. Change is the enemy, from the point of view of the PMBOK.

But change is inevitable (characteristic #12). If we try to restrict the client from making changes, then the software will be built without any consideration of what they learn about their needs during the course of the project. Even if we can build it exactly according to their initial specifications, by the

end they'll still be dissatisfied with the results. We may have fulfilled the letter
of the contract, but we won't have fulfilled the spirit of it, and that's how the
client will judge us.

When Should Scope Definition Occur?

ASSUMPTION Scope definition can be done before the project starts.

Another hidden assumption is that the scope definition process is sufficiently
uncomplicated that it can be performed outside the context of the project. We
define scope in order to obtain approval for activities that we hope to perform
during the course of a project. There's no point in including activities that have
already taken place.

However, for software development, scope definition can take up a substantial proportion of the project's duration and cost. At a Microsoft architecture workshop the author attended, one rule of thumb that met with universal
approval was that one-third of a project's effort should be devoted to requirements gathering.

Why should requirements gathering take up such a large proportion of
the project? Software is abstract (characteristic #2), so no money is spent on
raw materials or manual labor. The majority of the work is in obtaining the
requirements and then translating them into working software. Productivity
for the latter task is excellent because the repetitive work in software construction has been automated, so the requirements gathering takes up an unusually
large proportion of the project's time.

This issue is particularly challenging when the project is done under
contract. Generally, the client starts paying only when the contract has been
signed, so the cost of the scope definition is carried by the contractor. No contractor would be prepared to do a third of the work up front without guarantee
of payment, so this step is typically shortchanged. In the absence of any form
of ongoing scope definition, the consequences can be just as dire as the
PMBOK threatens.

Change control is a formal process in the PMBOK, which is understand-
able given the financial implications of uncontrolled scope expansion. After a
change is requested, variance analysis is carried out to determine its impact,
and it is then submitted for approval.

In practice, this approach doesn't work as expected. Either the change
control process is strictly enforced, in which case the stream of change
requests dwindles to virtually nothing, or the change requests increasingly
bypass the change control process. For software development, most of the
issues raised are to revise small details, so excessive bureaucracy is resented
and resisted.

But if the initial scope definition step is shortchanged, and if ongoing
scope definition is inhibited by a time-consuming change control process,

then at what stage can scope be properly defined? If clients and developers never have a chance to agree exactly what the goals of the project are, then what chance does the project have of achieving goals that are acceptable to both parties?

To be fair, the third edition of the PMBOK [PMI 2004] backs off from the hard-line pronouncements of the second edition [PMI 2000], and says that the "requirements will generally have less detail in the early phases, and more detail in later phases as the product characteristics are progressively elaborated. While the form and substance of the requirements will vary, it should always provide sufficient detail to support later project planning." The PMBOK, though, doesn't specify how to make this happen.

Time Management

This section discusses the four main activities in the area of time management in the sequence shown (Figure 3-1). They are performed after scope definition, and before resource planning and cost estimating (which will be discussed next).

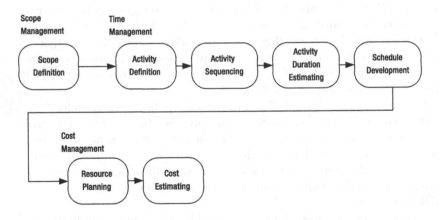

Figure 3-1. The main activities in scope, time, and cost management

Activity Definition

Activity definition is the first task in time management, and it occurs right after scope definition. Scope definition broke down the goals and requirements of the project into the Work Breakdown Structure hierarchy. Activity definition breaks down the work of the project into an activity list.

ASSUMPTION Software development consists of distinctly different activities.

Alongside software development, there's often a range of peripheral activities, such as configuring the production servers, training the users, and installing the software. Although these are valid and important tasks, let's put them to one side for a moment. Only rarely are they the reasons why software is late, faulty, and incomplete. So how many distinct activities are there in software development alone?

Although developers enjoy considerable variety in their work, there is nothing lengthy enough to be properly called an "activity." The only substantial activity that developers perform is software development itself. That's not what you'd expect from looking at the sample diagrams given in the PMBOK, which include activities such as design, code/construct, and unit test. To build software, or indeed to build any product, surely you need to first design it, then construct it, and finally test it? That seems to be the most logical and intuitive process to follow. Unfortunately, it's not what developers actually do.

Let's look over the shoulder of an expert developer on a typical day. She first picks a feature from her to-do list, and calls the client representative to confirm exactly how they'd like it to be implemented. Then she writes a set of small routines that test just that feature's functionality: this is called the *unit test*. After that, she might take a few minutes to discuss with her colleagues how the feature might best be implemented in the context of the whole system, perhaps by drawing a few rough diagrams on a whiteboard.

The remainder of the morning would be spent finishing the detailed design and writing the code, which together comprise a single activity (characteristic #10). As she writes the code, she adds comments in plain English to document how the feature works while it's still fresh in her mind. It takes a fraction of a second to run the unit test, and debugging continues until this test succeeds completely.

She then rebuilds the whole system, including the new feature, on her computer. All the other features and components already have their own unit tests, so integration testing is as simple as running that suite of tests. This may take a few seconds or a few minutes, depending on the size of the system. If any of the tests fail, then the new feature must have broken some of the existing functionality, and this bug must be fixed.

When the suite of tests succeeds completely, she uploads the updated code into the team's software repository. The task is finished. That night there will be an automatic rebuild and retest of all of the code in the repository to confirm that the whole system still works perfectly.

This description, complex though it is, still oversimplifies what really takes place. When he was researching the subject, Alistair Cockburn [1999] found that the "moment-to-moment process the team followed was so intricate that [he] couldn't possibly write it all down."

The developer may continue to talk to the client representative, discuss the design with her colleagues, run the unit test, and debug the code while she implements the new functionality. The unit test might be extended as she writes the code and discovers new ways in which the feature could fail.

One can argue that this task is actually a collection of distinct activities: we see the developer gathering requirements, writing a unit test, and integrating the feature into the rest of the system. However, given that the whole task is completed in a day or two, dividing the task up further would serve little purpose.

So what's the problem? Even if there's only one kind of activity, the project as a whole can still be broken down into a number of tasks. Our example shows what one of these tasks might involve.

The problem is that, although the activity definition could be done in this way, in practice it most often isn't. In both editions of the PMBOK discussed here [PMI 2000, 2004], there's a hidden assumption that software development consists of a set of distinctly different activities.

To a significant degree, this may come from the Deming Cycle (Figure 3-2), which is a concept that underlies many of the project management processes defined by the PMBOK. While there is no doubting the utility of this concept, it won't help project managers plan software development tasks that take only hours to complete.

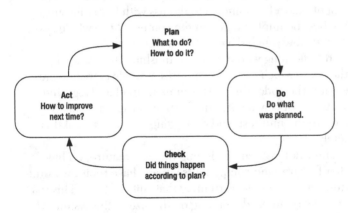

Figure 3-2. The Deming Cycle

Activity Sequencing

After defining the project's activities, the next step is to identify dependencies between them, and to sequence them so that each activity is performed only after the activities that it depends on have been completed. Activity sequencing is simple in the construction industry: rigid dependencies exist between various tasks. You can't roll tarmac before you've laid it, and you can't lay it before you've put down the foundations. However, this process is far more complex in the software industry.

ASSUMPTION Software development activities can be sequenced.

Software is commonly constructed in a number of "layers," each of which performs a different function. Figure 3-3 shows a common approach to structuring the layers. Someone who uses a program would interact with the *user interface*, which consists of the windows, menus, buttons, and fields that display the data and respond to the user's actions.

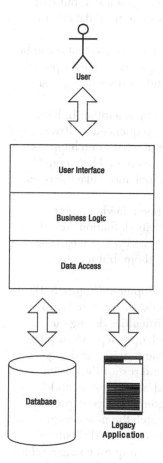

Figure 3-3. A typical software architecture

This functionality would normally be kept separate from the *business logic*, or middle layer of the application. For example, an insurance company might define business rules to calculate the premium for a driver from their driving history and the value of their car. These rules go into a separate layer so they can be used by any user interface screen that requires them.

The lowest layer is concerned with data storage and retrieval. It contains functionality to connect to a database or to an old *legacy* mainframe application that's too expensive to replace (such as inventory control). Each layer depends on the layers beneath it, so the user interface would depend on the business logic and data access layers, but not vice versa. You might expect that the lowest layer must be constructed first, and the highest layer last, but this is not the case. The layers can be constructed in any order.

For higher-level code, developers commonly use "stubs" to isolate the functionality from lower layers that haven't been written yet. A stub is a routine that appears to function just the way it should when you use it, but that doesn't actually do any real work. All it does is return some fixed data that allows code that uses it to be written and tested.

We saw earlier how a unit test can be written for a feature, so that it can be run without involving any of the other features in the program. This approach is often used to develop code in lower layers where the corresponding user interface isn't available yet.

By including activity sequencing, the PMBOK contains another hidden assumption, which is that activities can and should be sequenced. Software tasks have no intrinsic dependencies on each other. But what often happens in activity sequencing is that artificial dependencies are created between activities, just to make the activity sequence diagram look more like the ones printed in the PMBOK.

The worst situation occurs when the project has been divided up into design, construction, and testing activities during activity definition. Yes, these activities do have natural dependencies on each other, and yes, you can construct a neat and tidy activity sequence diagram from them, but no, this isn't a good way of doing things.

This is called the waterfall model of software development (Figure 3-4), because it's much easier going from one step to the next than it is to try to make your way back "upstream." If you encounter difficulties during one phase, then it's time-consuming and expensive to back up to a previous phase to fix them. If during construction, say, you find problems with the design, then the only option is to halt all construction work and restart the design process. Only after the new design has been finalized, documented, and signed off can construction start again. Most of the completed construction work will have to be thrown out because it doesn't match the new design.

This is particularly awkward because it makes changes very difficult to implement. We've seen how clients expect to be able to request changes (characteristic #12), and that, indeed, they must be able to request changes to compensate for the incompleteness of the requirements (characteristic #3). The waterfall model has no mechanism to allow them to do this, and it is therefore extremely inflexible.

Computer scientists often cite the waterfall model in order to use its flaws to justify their innovations. It has by now been thoroughly discredited. Few software development teams intentionally use it any more. So why mention it here? It's important to understand the waterfall model because teams often find themselves unintentionally mimicking it in their projects: the PMBOK can make waterfall development seem natural and appropriate. This is something to guard against.

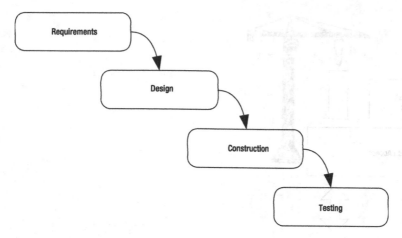

Figure 3-4. The waterfall model

Another issue is that each activity must produce an *artifact*—a tangible product such as a specification, plan, or other document—which will then be the input for the next activity in the sequence. Only the construction activity produces something that is actually useful to the client, which is the working software. The analysis, architecture, and design activities each produce a document that's used exactly once, and then is thrown away. This is an inefficient way to develop software.

A better approach is to sequence the activities so that lower layers are completed before work starts on the higher layers, building the application "from the ground up" (Figure 3-5). This avoids many of the problems of the waterfall approach, but it still introduces an artificial dependency that's unlikely to be justified. It's still onerous, although less so than for the waterfall model, to restart work on an already completed activity when problems are discovered during later work.

But the best way to organize the project is to ensure that the tasks with the highest level of risk are carried out first. That way, if, for example, a third-party component doesn't work as expected, then sweeping changes can be made to the system without having to rework a great deal of code that has already been completed. Mock-ups of the user interface can also fall into this category, as they help the client to identify missing or inaccurate requirements, which can then reduce risk later in the project.

What this means is that during each task the developer will make changes to several of the layers at once. This sounds like a recipe for disaster, but it isn't. It ensures that each layer works well with the others. There's no "big bang" integration phase at the end, where you try to pull all the pieces together but find that they don't quite fit.

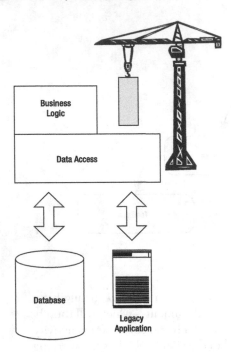

Figure 3-5. Building software "from the ground up"

Activity Duration Estimating

The third step in the time management process is activity duration estimating. It occurs right after activity sequencing. The individual activities are analyzed to estimate how long they will take. The PMBOK suggests that an estimate should originate from the individual most familiar with the nature of the specific activity.

ASSUMPTION There is always a way to produce meaningful estimates.

What happens if that person isn't on the team yet? The team is often assembled only after the project plan has been put together and approved, by which time it's too late to change the estimates that form the basis for the project's budget.

Quantitatively Based Durations

The PMBOK outlines three techniques to estimate the duration for activities. "Quantitatively based durations" is where you multiply the quantity of work (e.g., square meters of tarmac) by an average level of productivity. For well-known, repetitive tasks, this technique can produce the most accurate estimates. For example, in *Rapid Development*, Steve McConnell [1996] explains how to estimate a software schedule from the estimated number of lines of code in the finished software.

However, the data that he presents is based on software development projects in the 1970s and 1980s. Back then, the bulk of software development work was repetitive. There were no enterprise application frameworks, and almost all of the code was written from scratch.

Nowadays we expect that the majority of the work will have already been done for us, because we'll be using an enterprise application framework and a number of third-party components. We can only get the level of productivity we expect by reusing code that has already been written. An operation that requires at least 5,000 or 10,000 lines of code, if it has to be created manually, may take only 5 or 10 lines of code if a suitable tool or third-party component is available.

But whether a particular tool can do the job often depends on subtle distinctions in the client's requirements. This means that the lines of code and duration estimates can vary wildly, depending on whether the functionality has to be created from scratch.

Since technology experience is mostly out-of-date (characteristic #7), a large proportion of the tools will be new to the developers, and their applicability in a given context can only be determined by experience. All too often, this is by bitter experience, when a project exceeds its estimates due to unforeseen limitations and problems in the new technology.

Analogous Estimation

The second technique, "analogous estimation," uses the actual duration of previous, similar activities to estimate the duration of activities in the project that's being planned. It works best when there have been a number of projects that are similar in type and approach, if not in detail. Road building would be a good example of this.

"Analogous estimation is most reliable when a) the previous activities are similar in fact and not just in appearance, and b) the individuals preparing the estimates have the needed expertise," says the PMBOK [PMI 2000]. But for software development projects, neither of these conditions is likely to be true. If the previous software were sufficiently similar, then rather than using it as an example for estimation, its components and code would be reused directly in the current project. The schedule's accuracy would suffer, but this approach would offer considerable cost savings.

We've also discussed the extent to which software development is research (characteristic #8). You can only accurately determine how long it would take to solve a problem once you've solved that problem, and it's only at this point that the needed expertise becomes available.

Managers often ask developers how long it will take to fix a certain bug, or to fix all of the remaining bugs in the software. Any answer the developer gives is no more than a guess. Fixing a bug can take minutes, or it can take weeks. Until you've found it and fixed it, you can't tell which will be the case.

Expert Judgment

The last technique the PMBOK suggests is that of "expert judgment," which in practice means taking an educated guess. The PMBOK [PMI 2000] admits this when it says that "Expert judgment guided by historical information should be used whenever possible. If such expertise is not available, the estimates are inherently uncertain and risky." We've already seen how the rate of technology change makes technical experience date very quickly (characteristic #7), which makes suitable historical information difficult or impossible to obtain.

Estimating is always a difficult process, and one that introduces risk to a project. (Risk management will be covered in a later section.) However, in the PMBOK there does appear to be a hidden assumption that meaningful estimates can be produced by some means or other. What if this isn't possible? There's no provision in the PMBOK for planning projects that don't have such estimates.

What happens frequently in practice is that, under management pressure, developers come up with numbers with very limited validity, which are subsequently given far too much weight. When the project overruns these estimates, is the project going badly, or is it just the initial estimates that were at fault?

Interestingly, the third edition [PMI 2004] of the PMBOK glosses over this issue to a much greater degree than the second edition [PMI 2000], but its estimation process is still better suited to manual or machine-assisted physical labor.

Schedule Development

The activity duration estimates are used as an input to the schedule development task, which is the last step in the time management process. This is where a lot of the "heavy lifting" in project management is done, and a broad range of tools and techniques is available to plan and optimize a project's schedule.

> **ASSUMPTION** The size of the project team does not affect the development process.

Scheduling development for software projects should be very easy. Unless you've introduced the kinds of artificial dependencies that we discussed earlier, you can parallelize the tasks to your heart's content. That would get your new product into the marketplace awfully fast, wouldn't it? If five developers can develop the software in 10 weeks, then 50 developers could finish it in a week. Or could they?

The Mythical Man-Month is one of the most widely read computer science books. In it, Fred Brooks [1995] presents his central argument, which is that "large programming projects suffer management problems that are qualitatively different than small ones because of the division of labor; that the conceptual integrity of the software product is thus critical; and that it is difficult but possible to achieve this conceptual integrity."

What does this mean in real life? Software is complex (characteristic #1). The biggest challenge when developing software is to come to grips with its complexity, and to talk about it with other members of the team. Increasing the size of the team increases the size of the problem. That's obvious, but what might not be obvious is just how fast it grows.

Consider a team of three developers. Each developer has to be able to talk to every other developer. Andy and Beth talk to each other, Andy and Chang talk to each other, and Beth and Chang talk to each other. That's three communication paths.

But if you double the size of the team to 6 developers, then there are now 15 communication paths (Figure 3-6). Twelve developers have 66 communication paths, 24 developers have 276, and so on.

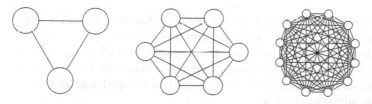

Figure 3-6. Communication paths in teams with 3, 6, and 12 members

It doesn't take long for communication to become the biggest overhead on the project. The more communication paths there are, the more room there is for misunderstandings between developers to creep in, and the more potential there is for bugs to arise. It's actually better, if somewhat counterintuitive, to limit the size of the team as much as possible in order to limit the communication overhead.

The hidden assumption here is that the only significant constraints on schedule development are the activity dependencies and resource availability, but team size and communication issues must also be taken into account. Moreover, because there's considerable overlap between the topics of schedule development and resource planning, there are additional related issues that are more relevant to the latter. These will be discussed in the next section.

Cost Management

This section covers the main activities in the area of cost management—resource planning and cost estimating. After discussing resource planning, we'll also be discussing two issues related to it: software documentation and developer productivity.

The two cost management tasks are the final steps toward completing a project plan. They build on the outputs from the scope management and time management processes.

Resource Planning

For software development, the most significant resources are the developers themselves. A server may cost a few thousand dollars, but even a small team of developers will cost hundreds of thousands of dollars per year. Software development resource planning is largely a process of assigning people to activities. Project managers use their judgment to assign the best available person to each task. Resource planning uses the results of, and occurs directly after, schedule development.

> **ASSUMPTION** Team members can be individually allocated to activities.

There's another hidden assumption here, which is that people can be individually and independently assigned to activities. We've already seen how the size of the team influences its level of communication overhead, but additional factors are also relevant here. The composition and structure of the team turns out to have a profound effect on how the software is developed, and thus on how good the resulting software is.

It takes time for team members to learn how to work together, and for a team to become more than the sum of its parts. Every project is unique, and every individual too, which is why it takes time to work out how best to organize them. A project manager can't arbitrarily swap people in and out, and expect the team to function just as well as it did before. This is true for any team, but it's particularly significant for software development teams.

One common approach is to specify a number of *roles*. In this context, a role is a specialization that someone might assume during a software development project: for example, architect, business analyst, programmer, or tester. Each role is given responsibility for a number of activities, and each role has one or more individuals assigned to it, who might have specific experience that suits them particularly for that role. This sounds very logical so far.

The problem is that by making such distinctions you increase the burden of communication on the team, and you also nudge the development process toward the flawed waterfall model. For example, testers wouldn't like the idea of being involved with coding, because they would have little or no experience with that activity, so they'd prefer to work with a version of the software that's essentially complete. Thus the testers would only join the team at a relatively late stage in the project.

But by coming on board at such a late stage, they'd then have to rapidly get up to speed on the project. They'd normally do this by asking their colleagues numerous questions, and by reading any existing documentation—but only if it proves to be particularly helpful. Nobody enjoys reading documentation. (We'll discuss the reasons for this in the next section.)

"Any manpower added to a late project makes it later." That's Fred Brooks's [1995] best-known slogan. There is a substantial burden on existing team members whenever someone new joins the team, simply due to the additional communication that's required to get them up to speed. Experienced developers know how true this is. Because software is so complex (characteristic #1), it takes time to learn how to find your way around the whole system.

Other background knowledge required by new team members includes

- The customer's requirements

- Project assumptions

- IT environment and systems

- The customer's culture

- Relationship history with the customer

- Contacts

Without a good understanding of these areas, it's easy to make costly and embarrassing mistakes.

The solution is to maintain continuity in the project team. Instead of continually interrupting the project to bring new team members on board, it's better to let the team acquire the knowledge it needs from day one. Let them gain familiarity with the scope of the project by gathering and analyzing the requirements themselves. Let the developers take a hand in designing the solution, so that they can better understand how the architecture fulfills its goals. Because software construction is actually a process of refining a design (characteristic #10), the more the developers understand the design, the more consistency and quality there will be in the code they write.

Developers don't just write code. They also do design work and perform testing. If you need to bring in an expert designer or tester, then bring them in to advise, guide, and train the team in their specialty. That way, the expertise stays with the team, rather than going straight out the door when the expert leaves.

You'll also find that team members will take a longer-term view if they know they'll have to use the results of their own work later in the project. It's hard to see how your work affects downstream activities, unless you've had firsthand experience of those activities and know which ideas help and which don't.

Software Documentation

Let's now take a look at the controversial topic of documentation. At first glance, documentation would appear to be the perfect solution for the previously mentioned issues in resource planning. If everyone properly documented their work, then wouldn't the communications overhead be eliminated? Instead of bothering their colleagues, new team members could get up to speed at their own pace. The documentation would become the repository of the team's knowledge, so it would stay with the team even when people left.

It's no wonder that documentation has traditionally been such a big part of the software development process. When managers try to increase the rigor of their software development projects, they typically demand an increase in the level of documentation. It's reassuring to get a hefty document at the end of each activity. It also makes project planning very easy: the output from one activity is the input to the next. Just assign any available person, and let them get on with the job.

There's only one problem: developers hate documentation. They hate reading it, and they particularly hate writing it. But is this just because they're lazy, or do they have a real justification? After all, developers are the ones who are expected to benefit from documentation, so they should be the first ones to see its benefits. Why don't they?

To properly discuss this topic, we must first realize that the question of whether to write documentation or not is actually a spurious one. The information must be conveyed one way or another, and there are a wide range of methods by which it can be communicated. A better question would be: which technique is the most appropriate to communicate this specific piece of information?

- We can speak face-to-face.

- We can videoconference.

- We can phone each other.

- We can exchange emails.

- We can write it up in a document.

Each of these methods has its own characteristics and limitations [Cockburn 2002]. By choosing to videoconference rather than speaking face to face, we remove physical proximity from the communication medium. Detail is obscured, and we lose many of the subliminal cues that we use to build rapport. Negotiation, problem solving, and brainstorming all become more difficult.

Moving from videoconferencing to phone, we lose visual gestures, expressions, and pointing. It's hard to keep track of exactly what the speaker is referring to. When we draw on a whiteboard, the actions of drawing and speaking serve to anchor and expand on each other. This is lost in a phone conversation.

In email there's no vocal inflection or timing. It's hard to get a sense of which ideas are more important, in what way they're being put forward, and exactly what the other person thinks about them. There's also a much more limited sense of dialogue: each communication stands on its own, and we don't have the immediacy and freshness of fully interactive communication.

Finally, for paper documentation we lose all interaction. The audience is unknown, so the writer must guess what topics, approach, and level of detail are suitable. They can't ask questions to check understanding, or accept questions to provide more explanation. There is no feedback.

From this it's clear that documentation is, in fact, the least rich and the least effective form of communication. The effort is greater and the results are worse than simply picking up the phone or stopping by to talk. It's no wonder that developers reject documentation as the way to communicate with one another.

What makes things even worse is that very often documentation is required as a thing in itself, for everyone and anyone, rather than for a specific audience. But if documentation is written for everyone, then it is written for no one. It becomes a dry assemblage of facts that's difficult and boring to read, rather than a pertinent set of solutions to the problems that face a specific individual or group.

There's no magic solution to the problem of knowledge management and communication. The most efficient approach is to make the person who uses the knowledge the same person as the one who discovered or created it. That way, there's no communications overhead and no chance of misunderstanding. Anything else is a compromise, and paper documentation is the greatest compromise of all. Excess documentation is actually a significant risk. Either too much time will be spent updating all the documents whenever anything changes, or the documents will become less and less useful as they get out of date.

Beyond the immediate project team, the situation is entirely different, and there is certainly a valid role for documentation. A project team works together for a period of time, and it has the flexibility to adjust its communication style as needed. However, when the project is over the team will be disbanded, and the team members may no longer be around to provide help and advice, but sources of information about the software will still be needed.

Users may require a "Getting Started" guide, for example, and the help desk may require a troubleshooting manual to resolve common problems. There are several distinct audiences that need specific information presented in specific ways. A skilled technical writer can produce effective documentation that addresses these particular audiences.

The hidden assumption here is that documentation is the best way to communicate information during a software project. The PMBOK doesn't specifically discuss this type of documentation, so this isn't a hidden assumption in project management, but it is important to understand how it relates to the other software project management issues.

Developer Productivity

ASSUMPTION One developer is equivalent to another.

The issue of developer productivity also affects resource planning. The assumption that resources can be individually allocated to activities carries with it the assumption that one developer can be substituted for another. The only exception is that senior developers are expected to be more productive than their junior colleagues.

Again, the truth is more complicated. Unlike, for example, construction workers, the productivity of individual software developers with similar levels of experience varies by a factor of at least ten to one. "Although specific ratios such as 25 to 1 aren't particularly meaningful, more general statements such as 'There are order-of-magnitude differences among programmers' are meaningful and have been confirmed by many. . . studies of professional programmers . . ." [McConnell 2004].

It takes a peculiar talent to work with the complexity and abstract nature of software. Some people exhibit prodigious talent, whereas others, who may be just as motivated and hardworking, continue to struggle. Moreover, individuals usually exhibit their ability in specific areas, such as detail work or client communication.

Barry Boehm [1981] makes the following recommendations in his seminal book *Software Engineering Economics*:

- "Top talent—Use better and fewer people."

- "Job matching—Fit the tasks to the skills and motivation of the people available."

- "Team balance—Select people who will complement and harmonize with each other."

A naive project manager who saw developers as equivalent to each other would be tempted to use the so-called "Mongolian Horde" approach, which uses a large number of cheap and inexperienced developers. Just as with the original Horde, the end result is chaos. Even allowing for their limited design and programming skills, the developers just don't have the experience to organize and deliver a system of this scale.

Some developers can even bring negative productivity to a team. They may not understand the sophistication of the team's code, and will introduce bugs that require lots of rework. They may demand so much help that their own work fails to compensate for the lost productivity of the other team members. Or their conflicting styles and difficult personalities may result in unproductive disagreements and reduced motivation all around.

Cost Estimating

ASSUMPTION Acceptably accurate estimates can be obtained.

The final issue to consider in the area of cost management is the dramatic disparity between the accuracy of cost estimates expected in project management and that which is available for software development according to industry research (Table 3-1). The project management figures originally came from the Association for the Advancement of Cost Engineering International, and are representative of the levels of contingency applied to projects in a wide range of industries.

Table 3-1. Accuracies of Estimates in Project Management and Software Development

Project Management Accuracy from the PMBOK Third Edition [PMI 2004]		Software Development Accuracy from Rapid Development [McConnell 1996]	
Conceptual	30% under to 50% over	75% under to 300% over	Initial product concept
Preliminary	20% under to 30% over	50% under to 100% over	Approved product definition
Definitive	15% under to 20% over	33% under to 50% over	Requirements specification
Control	10% under to 15% over	20% under to 25% over	Product design specification

What happens when a developer gives a single estimate instead of a range? The project manager will assume a level of variance in accordance with the left side of the table, but the true variance is actually that given on the right side of the table. Even if there is a contingency of 30 percent built into the project plan, the project may still be late and over budget when a slip of 50 to 100 percent occurs. The project can fail just because the contingency has been incorrectly calculated.

Why is there such a difference between these two sets of figures? We've seen that software development is a process of ongoing research to refine the customer's needs and discover the tools' capabilities (characteristic #8). Research is, by definition, an uncertain process: you don't know how long it will take to find out the unknowns until you've actually done so.

Quality Management

The main thrust of project planning goes through the sequence of scope, time, and cost management activities that we have just considered. Alongside these activities, however, project managers also spend some time planning their quality management and risk management strategies. These subjects will be briefly covered in the next two sections.

Metrics

According to the PMBOK, the two main tools that are created during the process of quality planning are the set of operational definitions (or quality metrics) and the set of quality checklists. "An operational definition defines, in very specific terms, what something is and how it is measured by the quality control process" [PMI 2000]. In other words, it's a metric. For example, the cookies produced at a bakery must be between 6.5 and 7.5 cm wide, or the electricity supplied by a distributor must be between 235 and 245 volts.

> **ASSUMPTION** Metrics are sufficient to assess the quality of software.

Aside from performance, the only real primary metric for software is the number and severity of the defects or bugs remaining in the software. The other metrics discussed in the literature are metrics for the process rather than the product: progress compared to plan, requirements changes over time, effort by activity, and so on. Still, it can be argued that the number of defects is all we need to measure. Clearly, if the program fails to work as intended, then this is not good. And if the software has no errors, then why shouldn't it pass quality assurance?

This approach may be suitable for other products, but it's too simplistic for software. We don't just expect the software to work as is; we also expect to be able to adapt and change it to meet our future needs (characteristic #12). We saw in the previous chapter how the quality of software shows up most clearly in its extensibility. Quality is more than just the absence of defects; it is also the fragility or robustness of the code.

Fragile code often generates new defects when it's modified; it's a breeding ground for bugs. Just finding and fixing those bugs won't be enough to resolve the broader problems in the design and implementation of the software. It will always be expensive and risky to maintain. There are no metrics to determine this when the software is first being written, which is when we'd really like to find it out. By definition, you can only test extensibility when you try to extend the system.

Before that point, the only option is to rely on subjective opinions of the elegance and flexibility of the design, and of the clarity and rigor of the code—hence the need for developers to review each other's designs and code. The hidden assumption is that the product measurements, and the metrics to which they belong, are sufficient inputs to the quality assurance process. This is clearly not true. By themselves, they don't give a complete enough view.

Despite this, metrics can still be valuable tools. Even if an application works properly, users will still complain if they find it to be too slow. It's therefore important to also monitor the application's average response time (its performance), and the number of concurrent users for which acceptable performance can be maintained (its scalability).

Secondary metrics include ease of use, productivity gains, and business benefits. These metrics are of critical importance, but they're very difficult to measure while the software is being developed. You have to put working software into the hands of real users for extended periods of time in order to get meaningful data.

Checklists

The other tool, the set of quality checklists, is even more problematic. According to the PMBOK, a checklist is "a structured tool, usually item specific, used to verify that a set of required steps has been performed," and it is employed "to ensure consistency in frequently performed tasks" [PMI 2000]. But we've seen that for software development, repetitive work is rapidly automated (characteristic #9). What's left is the problem solving, and every problem is unique. There are no significant "frequently performed tasks."

It's clear that software development requires quality assurance processes beyond those suggested in the PMBOK. Suggestions for additional quality assurance processes will be covered in Part Two.

It should be noted that the third edition of the PMBOK [PMI 2004] now accepts the inclusion of additional quality assurance activities in the quality management plan.

Risk Management

Finally, let's take a quick look at risk management. A project risk is an uncertain event or condition that has consequences for the project—for example, that poor weather will delay construction. The purpose of risk management is to identify, analyze, and respond to project risks. The PMBOK suggests four techniques for dealing with project risks:

- **Risk acceptance:** Allocate contingency time and/or funds that can be used to absorb the impact if one of the risks eventuates.

- **Risk transference:** Assign responsibility for the risks to another party.

- **Risk avoidance:** Find alternative processes that do not include these risks.

- **Risk mitigation:** Find ways to make the risks less likely to eventuate, or to reduce the impact when they do.

Risk Acceptance

Risk management deals with known risks, that is, risks that can be foreseen.
A typical risk register for a software development project would include

1. The requirements are incomplete, and the project scope will change.

2. The tools and third-party components don't work as expected.

3. The developers lack sufficient skills and expertise.

4. The software developed will have flaws that require rework.

5. Sickness, resignations, and other projects will reduce the number of people available to work on this project.

The risks in software development seem to be easy to identify. We've discussed most of these risks in previous sections. However, at this level the risk descriptions are so generic as to be almost useless. Any risk evaluation at this level would be little more than a guess. But difficulties arise as soon as we try to drill down into these categories.

Let's examine them one by one:

1. We know that the requirements will be incomplete (characteristic #3), and that change is inevitable (characteristic #12). This risk has a 100 percent chance of eventuating. However, how can we predict what the client will learn about their needs during the development process? We can only wait for them to tell us. Moreover, any changes to the scope could introduce new risks: how can you plan for these before you know what they are?

2. The process of development is one of problem solving (characteristic #8): we find ways to implement the functionality required by the client. When you're solving a problem, you don't know how you're going to solve that problem until you've actually done it, and you don't know which features of your tools will be needed to help you do so. How can we estimate what impact this will have? A limitation in a tool or component may require a one-line workaround, or it may require thousands of lines of additional code to reproduce the functionality that is required.

3. Technical experience goes out-of-date very quickly (characteristic #7), so it's virtually certain that the project will introduce new tools, components, and features that the developers haven't used before. But until you've learned enough about them, how can you determine how long it will be before you can use them effectively?

4. All software has bugs. Yes, even computer science luminary Donald Knuth, who was so confident in his TeX page layout program that he offered cash rewards to people who found bugs, has had to pay out again and again over the years. A bug may take a minute to find and fix, or it may take a week.

5. This is the one exception to the pattern. Over time we can measure sick days, employee turnover, and project contention to obtain well-founded estimates for these factors. This risk is specific and measurable.

Software development is a process of research (characteristic #8). The intrinsic risk of research is that what you find out happens to be more complicated than you thought it could be, and this risk can't be quantified. You can't predict how complicated the problem or the solution will eventually become.

To be fair, the PMBOK also allows for qualitative risk analysis, where the impact of the risk on the project is rated as Very Low, Low, Moderate, High, or Very High. But without better knowledge of the risks at hand, even these evaluations are likely to be little better than guesswork.

"Unknown risks cannot be managed, although project managers may address them by applying a general contingency based on past experience with similar projects," says the PMBOK [PMI 2000]. For our five risks, although we can name them, we know very little about them. Does this mean that the risk management process is useless for software development?

It is if we follow it blindly. The level of contingency is often limited by quantitative estimates that may be wildly inaccurate. Contingencies are typically too small, as we saw earlier, except where teams have learned otherwise through painful experience.

Risk Transference

Risk acceptance is only one of the strategies that the PMBOK puts forward for risk response planning. For any given organization, risk transference is another option, but responsibility has to be assigned somewhere. It could be assigned to the customer, to the contractor, or to a subcontractor, but the recipient still has to manage the risk.

Unfortunately, there's no software development equivalent to the completion bonds that are a common way to manage risk in the film and construction industries. A completion bond is an insurance policy that guarantees completion of the project, which means that none of the participants are responsible for the risk. A software completion bond would be a useful option, if it were ever introduced.

Risk Avoidance

For the reasons outlined previously, the kinds of risks that are common to software development projects can't feasibly be avoided. For example, some contracts attempt to prevent the client from making any changes, but this situation rarely ends well. And you can look for developers who know everything about everything that's relevant to your project, but you're unlikely to find them.

Risk Mitigation

The last strategy recommended by the PMBOK is that of mitigation, which "seeks to reduce the probability and/or consequences of an adverse risk event to an acceptable threshold" [PMI 2000]. Given that software projects tend to share the same sets of risks, we can find mitigation responses that are applicable to software development projects in general. We'll discuss the mitigation responses pioneered by the new agile methodologies in Chapter 5, but be warned: they usually involve breaking PMBOK rules.

The risk management model in the PMBOK is comprehensive and useful, and it seems that there are no specific hidden assumptions that prevent it from being used in software projects. However, software projects exhibit unique characteristics that make it difficult to apply, and it is often applied badly. After all, would such numbers of projects have failed so badly if their risks had been properly managed?

Summary

In this chapter we've taken a crucial step toward understanding why software projects fail. Our analysis of project management has revealed ten hidden assumptions that don't appear to be valid for software development projects. In the next chapter we'll take this a step further by working through a case study that shows how these assumptions can cause problems for software projects and examines the impact that each of them can have:

1. Scope can be completely defined.

2. Scope definition can be done before the project starts.

3. Software development consists of distinctly different activities.

4. Software development activities can be sequenced.

5. Team members can be individually allocated to activities.

6. The size of the project team does not affect the development process.

7. There is always a way to produce meaningful estimates.

8. Acceptably accurate estimates can be obtained.

9. One developer is equivalent to another.

10. Metrics are sufficient to assess the quality of software.

Case Study: The Billing System Project

In the previous chapter we performed an in-depth analysis of project management to discover where it breaks down for software development. This chapter covers the same issues, but from a different perspective. It introduces a fictional case study (the same scenario as the one that begins the Introduction) to illustrate how the ten hidden assumptions come into play, and how they lead to the problems that cause projects to fail. At the end of the chapter we will consider what impact each of the assumptions had.

The case study is not necessarily a typical project, since many aspects have been simplified for reasons of clarity and space, but it is by no means unusual. Each of the issues in the case study has occurred in at least one real-life project that the author has been involved with.

This is the last chapter in Part One. In Part Two we'll try to find solutions for these issues, building on the ideas that we have already discussed. Part Two will finish with another case study that reworks this scenario to show how it could have succeeded had the project been managed differently.

Requirements

Acme Inc.—a medium-sized toy manufacturer—has seen its stock price slide significantly over ongoing losses from its expansion program. Each department has been asked to cut its costs by 10 percent to help profitability and reassure investors. Karen, the accounting manager, has come up with the idea of integrating the various financial applications that are used by her team, so that the data would be entered only once into a new master application, which would then automatically copy it into the other applications. Her department could shed three full-time data-entry roles by eliminating multiple entry of the same data.

Karen went to see her boss Salim, who, as the chief financial officer, had the authority to approve or reject the project. He liked the idea, but urged caution: "Remember, we're trying to save money, so we've got to keep the cost of the project down. Company policy says that any new investment has to pay for itself within three years. Given the position that the company's in right now, I'd like to see payback well before then. See what you can do."

Salim contacted Acme's preferred employment agency, People Co., to hire an experienced business analyst as a contractor for two weeks to scope and estimate the project. Brian came on board a week later, and immediately set up a series of meetings with Karen to go over the requirements. By the end of the two weeks, he had completed a thick functional specification document. He had also come up with an initial estimate of $300,000 for the whole project, including $7,500 for his work so far.

This figure relieved both Karen and Salim, as the expected savings were around $150,000 per year, so the investment would be fully recouped within two years. The project was given the go-ahead to begin planning.

Planning

While Acme has outsourced all of its IT needs, it does still have a number of capable and experienced operational project managers on its staff. After chatting to the operations manager, Salim found out that one of his subordinates—Phil—happened to have some free time over the coming months, and that he could certainly take responsibility for the new project.

Phil spent a week going over the estimates and scope that Brian had written up, and in his project plan he organized the duration, resource, and cost estimates (Table 4-1).

Table 4-1. Duration, Resource, and Cost Estimates for the Project's Activities

Activity	Resources	Name(s)	Duration	Cost
	Project sponsor	Salim	N/A	N/A
	Key business owner	Karen	N/A	N/A
Requirements	1 business analyst	Brian	½ month	$7,500
Design	1 software architect	Angela	1 month	$20,800
Construction	4 developers	Reiko, Tim, Hua, Mike	2½ months	$138,600
System Testing	1 tester	Ian	½ month	$6,100
User Testing	1 end user	Emily	½ month	$4,300
Rework	4 developers	(as above)	½ month	$27,700
Project Management	½ project manager	Phil	4 months	$34,700
TOTAL				$239,700

He divided the remainder of the project into Design, Construction, and Testing/Debug phases (Figure 4-1).

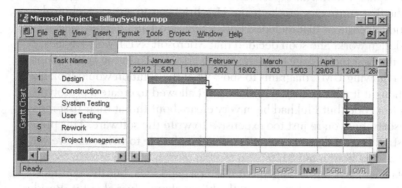

Figure 4-1. The overall project plan

Phil also considered which risks were most likely to affect the project (Table 4-2). He followed the common practice of multiplying together the probability and impact of each risk to obtain a figure for how much contingency was needed. The impact of sickness could be ignored since Acme didn't pay for the contractors' sick leave, and because he thought that one end user could easily be substituted for another. After adding 10 percent contingency for unknown risks, Phil ended up with what he thought was a generous contingency reserve of 25 percent for the project as a whole.

Table 4-2. The Risk Register

Billing System Project Risks	Probability	Impact	Contingency
Changes to requirements.	20%	25%	5%
Problems integrating with existing systems.	25%	20%	5%
Developers not as competent as expected.	10%	20%	2%
The system will be more buggy than expected.	30%	10%	3%
Sickness will delay the project.	10%	0%	0%
Unknown risks will arise.			10%
TOTAL			25%

The final estimates for the project's cost and duration were $299,600 and five months respectively, and, as the formal sponsor for the project, Salim was happy to sign off on it.

Design

People Co. quickly found an experienced software architect, and Angela became the first contractor on the team. Her brief was to write a technical specification document that included both a high-level architecture and detailed design work. She soon decided that Microsoft .NET web services would be the best technology to connect the various accounting applications, and began drawing UML diagrams to show what the solution would look like.

She thought it a bit strange that she wasn't allowed to create a prototype or write any test code, but Phil had been very clear about this at their first meeting. "I'm sorry, but you're just too expensive to write the software. This project is under strict financial constraints. There's a lot of code to write, and we want it done at $80 an hour—not $120."

Angela knew that this arrangement wasn't a good idea, but this contract was only for a month, and it wasn't worthwhile making a fuss about it. Besides, it wouldn't be her problem when things went awry.

Construction

As soon as Angela had decided on the basic technology, Phil went back to People Co. to look for developers with the corresponding skills. He didn't want novices who couldn't be trusted to deliver the results, but he didn't want anyone too expensive either. People Co. was able to find four intermediate-level developers who claimed familiarity with .NET and web services: Reiko, Tim, Hua, and Mike.

On Monday morning, the four developers turned up to find that they had been given spare offices in various parts of the Acme building, one of which had just been vacated by Angela. They quickly got busy installing their development software and reading the two thick specification documents that Phil had given them.

"We'll have team meetings every two weeks," he said to them, "but in the meantime if you encounter any issues or problems, then don't hesitate to come and talk to me about them. My door is always open."

Over coffee that afternoon the developers decided to divide the work into four big chunks: the user interface and business logic, the database, the web service interfaces, and the infrastructure. Hua had worked on a couple of big database projects, so she volunteered to look after the database access functionality. Reiko took over the user interface and business logic, Tim got the web service interfaces, and Mike was left with the infrastructure. They decided to work individually for two months, and then spend the last two weeks bringing all the pieces together.

Coding

Before long, Reiko discovered that the functional specification didn't actually describe how the new application's screens should be laid out. She asked Phil about this.

"Brian said that these requirements would be all that you'd need to build the user interface," was his response. "Why don't you just put together something reasonable, and then update the functional specification to document what you've done?"

Reiko had hoped that she could get away with just writing the code, but she accepted in good grace. When she realized that the error messages hadn't been specified either, she didn't bother to ask Phil, but just made them up herself, and then added them to the functional specification too.

On the other side of the building, Tim was having real difficulties. He had worked on a web services project before, so he was comfortable accepting responsibility for the web services interfaces. However, some of the accounting applications had peculiar requirements for the format of their data, and the interfaces that the .NET tools were creating just didn't work.

He discovered that, rather than relying on his tools to create the interfaces, he would have to create them by hand from technologies he knew nothing about. However, he knew that books about these technologies were easy to find, so he kept quiet and hoped that he could learn enough to get it all done in time.

As Mike started work on the program's internal infrastructure, he realized that the design, although elegant, needed some refinement to allow it to do everything that was needed. In fact, it really could do with a substantial makeover. However, when he mentioned the problem to Phil, his response wasn't very encouraging:

"Angela came highly recommended as a software architect, and I don't want you to change her design any more than is absolutely necessary. I also want you to document precisely what changes you do make. The technical specification is the documentation for this software, and I want it to be complete and accurate at all times."

So instead of the redesign that Mike thought was necessary, he was reduced to putting in a series of quick and ugly fixes for all of the functionality that was missing in the infrastructure design.

At the project meetings, each developer reported steady progress, with another 25 percent completed every two weeks. "Well, it looks like we're staying on track," said Phil.

Integration

After two months, the team got back together to integrate their code. Going around the table, they found that each person's work was pretty much complete. Reiko spoke for everyone when she said, "My code is still a bit rough around the edges. It should work fine, but the error handling, for example, could do with a bit more work. I'm sorry, but updating all the documentation has made everything take twice as long."

However, when they tried to compile together the four separate chunks of the system, it failed with a very long list of error messages. They worked throughout the day to sort them out, but it seemed that for every one they fixed, two more would appear. By the end of the day, the list was starting to shrink again, but Hua was still quite panicky:

"You guys go home. I'll stay here. We can't all work on this at the same time anyway. We haven't got long to get it working properly, and the least I can do is to get it to compile."

However, the work went very slowly, and at 2 A.M. Hua gave up with half a dozen serious errors remaining. What was worse, though, was that she had noticed a fundamental incompatibility between Reiko's business logic and Tim's web services. She called the team together for a meeting as soon as they came in the next morning. The mood was tense.

"Guys, we've got a big problem. Reiko has written her code to use transactions, but Tim's web services don't support transactions," she said.

"It has to use transactions," said Reiko. "It's in the functional spec. The updates to the database and the updates via the web services have to either all work perfectly, or all be aborted together. Without transactions, how else can you abort one update when another one fails?"

"But web services don't support transactions yet," said Tim. "That technology has been delayed again, and it won't be out until the beginning of next year."

"Is there a workaround?" asked Mike.

"I think so, yes," said Hua. "For every web service, we can add another web service to undo that update. Then if we need to abort the transaction, we just call that undo web service."

"But that means doubling the size of the web service module," said Tim. "There's no way I can finish all of that in the next two weeks."

"Reiko and I will help you," said Mike. "Hua can finish up the integration; she's been doing really well on that so far. But we really need to get everything done before we have to hand it over to the testers. Is there any way that we can get things done faster?"

"Lose the documentation," said Tim immediately. "That's the biggest overhead. Every time I make the slightest change to the code, I have to spend a lot of time updating all the diagrams. I know it's nice to have good documentation, but surely it's a lower priority than getting the system working properly?"

"OK. And no gold plating either. I don't care if it's a bit rough and ready, but it all has to be in place by a week from Monday," said Mike.

The last two weeks were a nightmare. Hua was able to get the program to compile at last, but it immediately crashed when she tried to run it. It was hard tracking down the bugs because each of the developers had written their code in a very different style. The code had few comments, and it was difficult to understand how it worked.

"Oh well," she thought to herself, "we've still got the Debug phase ahead of us. It'll be much easier when we can all work on our own code again."

The web service undo code turned out to be trickier than they had expected, and it still wasn't quite complete by the last Friday, so the developers decided to work through the weekend. At the handover meeting on Monday morning, they were at least able to claim that the software was now "feature complete," even if it still had a few bugs. It was now in the hands of the tester, Ian, and Emily, the end user from the accounting team.

Testing

The first bug report came in just ten minutes after the handover meeting, and after that they flooded in. Over the rest of that week, the bug list grew to include over 160 serious or critical bugs. On Friday, Phil called a meeting to discuss the situation.

"We were planning to deploy the system in a week's time," he said. "I really need to know whether we can still make that date."

Hua shook her head. "We've fixed nearly 60 bugs this week, which is a tremendous rate, but there's no way that we can get the rest done by the end of next week. We'll need another week, maybe two to be on the safe side."

"Well, buggy code was one of the risks I identified at the beginning of the project, and that's what the contingency is for. I'm comfortable pushing back the release date by two weeks," replied Phil.

"I'm not," said Ian. "There are a lot of features that I can't test yet because the program fails before I can even get to that point. I'm sure that there are still a lot more bugs to be found."

"That's because half of the bug reports are actually change requests," replied Reiko. "Look at this: 'Can't paste a block of data from a spreadsheet into the table.' That's not in the functional specification."

"It's what we do at the moment," said Emily. "I thought this software was supposed to save us time, not make our work slower. If we have to copy over one number at a time, then we'll spend twice as long on each invoice."

"OK, guys," said Phil, "let's slip the date by three weeks, but I really want you to make sure it's done by then. I'd like to keep that last week of contingency time for any issues arising from the deployment. Reiko, I see your point, but the accounting guys have to be OK with the software too. I want you to work with Emily to find the minimum set of changes that will keep them happy. Tim, you work with the developers so they can fix the bugs that are holding back your testing. And I want another project meeting in a week's time."

At the next project meeting the developers were ranged down one side of the table, and the testers down the other. Each side glared at the other.

Reiko was the first to speak. "Emily hasn't backed down on any of her change requests. In fact, she's added more. At this rate the software will never be finished."

"I talked it over with Karen, and with the rest of my team, and they all agree with me," replied Emily. "We need software that we can use. Karen's not going to switch us over to the new system until we're 100 percent happy with it."

"Let's talk about that in a moment. How's your end doing, Ian?" asked Phil.

"Sorry, Phil, it's not going well. The guys have managed to open up most of the application, but it seems like every time they fix one bug they break two more things. The number of serious and critical bugs is now 230."

"I'm still confident that we can make the deadline," said Hua. "I think we've fixed most of the really hard bugs, so the rest should go faster."

Phil thought for a moment. "I'm willing to give you the whole month's contingency to fix those bugs, and to make the changes that the accounting guys require. But that's the absolute deadline. This project is supposed to save money. There's no way that I'm going to let it go over budget."

Death March

The developers worked as fast as they could for the next four weeks, but it became increasingly apparent that they just couldn't make the deadline. The bug list had stopped growing, but it wasn't shrinking fast enough, and every new feature that Reiko and Tim finished added its share of bugs to the total.

At the five-month mark, Phil finally allowed the project to slip beyond its planned contingency. He rationalized that it was better to accept a small loss than to throw away everything they'd worked so hard for.

Mike left the team at about the same time. He'd become increasingly unhappy as the project got into more and more trouble, so he arranged another contract to start as soon as the one with Acme was due to expire. He was replaced at short notice by Deepak, a recent graduate who had studied .NET at college.

However, Deepak found it very hard to work on the software. The code had had so many hasty changes that it was disorganized and messy, and the documentation was so out-of-date that it was almost useless. He alternated between spending hours peering over the shoulders of the other developers and spending hours in his own office making very little progress and getting increasingly frustrated.

Aftermath

The release date kept slipping, and eventually both Salim and the CEO, Cathy, got involved. Salim asked Angela to return to Acme to provide solid estimates for all the "essential" changes that Emily had asked for. Angela suggested that they allow another month for these changes.

At the six-month mark, the project was already 30 percent over budget, and it needed at least another 60 percent to complete, including a month's work to clear up the remaining bugs (Figure 4-2). Cathy had no hesitation in canceling the project.

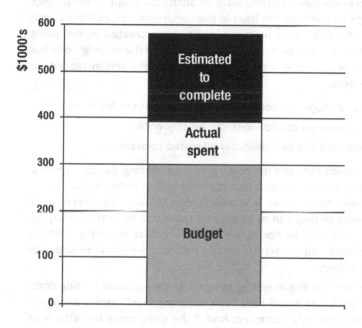

Figure 4-2. The financial position when the project was canceled

"This project is in very bad shape, and there's no guarantee that it will ever be completed successfully. I'm just not willing to put any more money into it."

Salim lost his bonus over this project, and Phil missed out on the promotion that he had been expecting. Both were chastened by the experience, but neither of them really understood where the project had gone wrong.

Summary

So where did the project go wrong? If we compare the case study to the list of project management assumptions we identified in Chapter 3, we can see that most of the problems in the project occurred because the project plan relied on these assumptions, and because they turned out to be incorrect:

1. Scope can be completely defined.

2. Scope definition can be done before the project starts.

There was no opportunity to reevaluate or adjust the scope of the project. Emily was right to point out the flaws in the requirements, but she was only able to do so after all of the functionality had been created. At this point, the changes to the requirements meant that some of the existing code had to be thrown away and rewritten, which was wasteful and increased the cost of the project.

3. Software development consists of distinctly different activities.

4. Software development activities can be sequenced.

5. Team members can be individually allocated to activities.

The lack of overlap between the requirements gathering, design, construction, and testing activities meant that communication between the individuals performing these tasks was extremely limited. The specification documents were all they had to go on, and there was no way to ask questions or give feedback. The developers couldn't discuss the design with the software architect, and the testers couldn't discuss the requirements with the business analyst.

If the developers had begun testing as soon as they started writing code, then the quality issues would have been apparent much earlier, and could have been systematically addressed. And if the developers had also been responsible for the design of the software, then it could have been refined as required once they were able to see how the software was shaping up.

6. The size of the project team does not affect the development process.

The team was very small, and could have worked more efficiently by adopting a less formal development process. Face-to-face conversation is a much less laborious way to communicate information than via documentation.

7. There is always a way to produce meaningful estimates.

8. Acceptably accurate estimates can be obtained.

9. One developer is equivalent to another.

The project was estimated before the team members were identified, so no allowance was made for individual variations in skill—such as Tim's limited knowledge of web services. The team had never worked together before, so there was no way to check the estimates against the outcomes of earlier projects. In hindsight it's obvious that the contingency reserve of 25 percent was grossly inadequate.

10. Metrics are sufficient to assess the quality of software.

The team used two metrics to assess their progress. In the Construction phase they estimated the proportion of the functionality that they had completed. In the Testing phase they counted the number of bugs that had been reported. The sheer number of bugs made it clear that the software was of low quality, but this metric misled the team into believing that fixing these bugs would be enough to fix the software. But the more frantically they worked on the software, the more messy and fragile it became. Their efforts just reduced the quality even further.

…AND HOW TO MAKE THEM SUCCEED

5

The New Agile Methodologies

In Part One we saw how naively applied project management practices can derail software projects run by even the most capable project managers. Is the solution to throw out half of project management's best practices and hope for the best?

The case study helped us to understand how poor quality can bring down a software development project. But solutions are available. Over the last five to ten years, several new software development methodologies have been developed specifically to resolve the issues around software quality. These methodologies are called "agile" because they aim to maximize flexibility and minimize overhead in the process of software development (see the agile manifesto in the Appendix). They're not based on theory, but rather derived from the experiences of successful project teams.

Sabre's recent successful rewrite of its 25-year-old air-travel reservation system shows how agile practices can improve the outcome of software projects: "Sabre has tried to overhaul its reservation system before—most infamously from 1988 to 1992, when it spent $125 million on a megaproject to do just that. A few weeks ahead of the promised completion date, Sabre had to junk the entire system.

"So what makes this new four-year, $100 million-plus success different from that old four-year, $100 million-plus catastrophe? This time, it wasn't a big leap. Borrowing techniques from so-called agile programming, Sabre did it as a series of small steps. . . . As a result, the system already looks a lot different now than the design did in 2001, when the project started. Small steps—and a willingness to change direction—make that possible" [Hayes 2004].

This experience isn't unusual. "Companies adopting agile processes are happy," writes Forrester analyst Liz Barnett. "We've seen quite a number of successes and, quite frankly, have yet to meet an agile failure" [Cooney 2004].

The new methodologies will form part of our proposed solution for the problems outlined in Part One. Despite this, they aren't a complete solution: even with high-quality software, a project can still fail if its deadlines and budget are incorrectly calculated. In the next chapter we'll look at ways to resolve this issue, and thereby bridge the gap between the agile methodologies and traditional project management.

Selected Methodologies

Agile methodologies help developers create better software more easily. To discover how they do this, let's first take a detailed look at three specific agile methodologies to find out how they work:

- Crystal

- Extreme Programming

- The Rational Unified Process

We'll use Crystal to introduce the subject because, even though it's a flexible and capable methodology in its own right, it presents the key agile concepts in a clear and straightforward manner. Then we'll take a look at Extreme Programming (XP)—perhaps the best-known and most popular of the agile methodologies. XP shares many ideas with Crystal, but it has its own priorities and unique approach. We'll finish up with the Rational Unified Process (RUP), which is an industry-standard methodology toolkit that has been used for even the largest and most complex projects. Depending on how it's used, RUP can be very agile, or it can be completely non-agile.

Each of these methodologies has its own series of books, so the summaries given here are limited. This chapter aims to highlight only the main ideas, and show how they address the software quality problems described in Part One.

After describing these methodologies, the next step is to see how they solve the problems that project management can't. In Chapter 3, we discovered that risk management in software projects is especially difficult. Taking Crystal and XP as our examples, we'll show how they address the five specific risks that software development projects typically face.

At the end of the chapter we'll relate the agile methodologies to the ten hidden assumptions we identified in Chapter 3, to show how they avoid the problems that typically bedevil software development project management.

Other Agile Methodologies

Other well-known methodologies that aren't described in this book, but which may be of interest, include the following:

- Adaptive Software Development [Highsmith 1999]

- Dynamic System Development Method (DSDM) [Stapleton 2003]

- Evolutionary Project Management (EPM or Evo) [Gilb 1989]

- Feature-Driven Development (FDD) [Palmer and Felsing 2002]

- Lean Software Development [Poppendieck 2003]

- Microsoft Solutions Framework (MSF) [Microsoft 2003]

- OPEN Process Framework [Firesmith and Henderson-Sellers 2001]

- SCRUM [Schwaber and Beedle 2001]

Crystal

Alistair Cockburn is the most humble of the methodologists. His Crystal methodologies come directly from years of interviewing teams to find out how they succeeded. He found that they largely ignored the formal methodologies that they'd inherited, but delivered software successfully anyway. Crystal is his attempt to formulate and describe what it was that they actually did that worked so well.

As a result, the Crystal methodologies are the most descriptive, and the least prescriptive, of the lot. They particularly emphasize tolerance of individual variation: each team interviewed did things slightly differently, yet they all succeeded. This makes Crystal particularly palatable and easy to apply. "Crystal . . . aims to be a simple and tolerant set of rules that puts the project into the safety zone" [Cockburn 2004].

This focus on tolerance comes from Cockburn's [1999] research into people's behavior in teams:

- "People are communicating beings, doing best face-to-face, in person, with real-time question and answer."

- "People have trouble acting consistently over time."

- "People are highly variable, varying from day to day and place to place."

- "People generally want to be good citizens, are good at looking around, taking initiative, and doing 'whatever is needed' to get the project to work."

These characteristics are why methodologies like Crystal avoid the rigid process definitions that were so prevalent in older methodologies. A process that can be represented on a flow chart is one that treats developers like mechanical components that perform fixed tasks over and over again. Human beings can work this way, but they're not very good at it. They function best when they can use their initiative and flexibility to adapt to an ever-changing situation.

Cockburn realized that teams of different sizes need different strategies to manage their particular problems. He developed a family of methodologies to take account of these variations, which includes Crystal Clear for 2 to 8 developers, Crystal Yellow for 9 to 20, Crystal Orange for 21 to 50, and so on. The following seven properties are common to all of the methodologies:

1. Frequent delivery

2. Reflective improvement

3. Close or osmotic communication

4. Personal safety

5. Focus

6. Easy access to expert users

7. Technical environment with automated tests, configuration management, and frequent integration

They are identified as properties, rather than principles or procedures, because of Cockburn's project evaluations. He discovered that projects that had more of these properties tended to succeed more often.

1. Frequent Delivery

An *iteration* is a small part of a project that contains all of the steps required to design and build a portion of the software. It starts by choosing a set of features to add during the course of the iteration. The high-level design is extended and adjusted to accommodate the new features. Once the features have been developed and tested, the developers can integrate and evaluate an updated version of the software.

The idea of developing software in a series of iterations is common to all of the agile methodologies, but Crystal goes even further than that. It requires the delivery of running, tested code to the users on a regular basis, from weekly to quarterly depending on the length of the project and the ease of deployment.

Iterations are important to avoid the situation, illustrated in the case study, where the status of the software becomes apparent only at the very end of the project, when it's too late to do anything about it. By integrating and testing the software on a more frequent basis, you ensure that problems can be discovered and resolved at an earlier stage, before they have a chance to grow too big.

With each iteration, the project's sponsors get solid information about the progress of the project. The developers get a morale boost from seeing visible progress, and they also have an opportunity to evaluate and optimize their development processes, including the process of deployment.

The most important benefit is the opportunity to get feedback from the users, which is why Crystal insists that real software should be delivered to real users. We've seen how difficult it is to create a clear and comprehensive set of requirements upfront, and that doing so removes flexibility from the project.

Frequent delivery allows the team to refine the project's scope and fill in the gaps, based on real experience of the product under development. The client has an opportunity to say "That's not what I meant," or change their mind when they see the results of their decisions. The software can then better address the client's needs.

Crystal distinguishes between an iteration, where the software is built to the point where it could be released, and a delivery where the software is actually released to users (Figure 5-1). It may not be practical to deploy new versions of the software to the users as often as the team would like, but iterations can be as frequent as desired, to obtain as much benefit from them as possible.

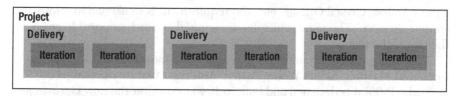

Figure 5-1. The deliveries and iterations in a typical Crystal project

2. Reflective Improvement

Most software projects get off to a rocky start. It's hard to predict what strategies will work best for the unique circumstances of a project team before you begin to accumulate real experience. Many troubled projects have gone on to eventual success because the team took time out from their day-to-day development work to think about how to improve or fix their processes.

One of the benefits of using iterations is that they provide a natural rhythm for these reviews. Another is that the process for finishing up the iteration provides important feedback on how well, or how badly, the project is progressing.

Crystal encourages teams to hold a "reflection workshop" every few weeks to identify the practices, conventions, and habits that work, and to find alternatives for the ones that don't. The team can test different strategies until they find one that works for them.

This reflection workshop isn't intended to substitute for iteration planning and review meetings, but reflection could also occur in those meetings if the team is encouraged to contribute issues and suggestions in them.

You should expect or even welcome the problems that come up in these reviews because, as Cockburn [2004] says, "from that first catastrophe comes all sorts of new and important information about the project's working environment, information that would otherwise be just as deadly, but hidden, lurking."

This approach addresses most of the problems identified in previous chapters. After all, problems rarely go away by themselves, and to fix a problem you first must be aware of it. Unless a project's budget and deadline are wildly incorrect, most of the project plan can be adjusted to suit the situation as it eventuates.

Interestingly, Crystal doesn't specify the format of the reflection workshop. This could also evolve as the team gains experience with its processes.

3. Close or Osmotic Communication

Crystal Clear requires "osmotic communication," where the whole team is seated in the same room so that information flows effortlessly between them "as though by osmosis" [Cockburn 2004]. For teams larger than six to eight people, the environment can become increasingly noisy and distracting, so for Crystal Yellow, Crystal Orange, etc., the requirement is weakened to "close communication." The same principles are applied as much as possible given the size of the team.

This idea has been around for a long time. The most famous example was Lockheed Martin's "Skunk Works," where America's first production jet aircraft (the P-80) was designed and built in 1943 to counter the new German jet fighters during World War II. Team members attributed the tremendous pace and success of the project to the degree of overcrowding, where you were literally rubbing shoulders with your colleagues.

In this environment, information flows rapidly and easily between the members of the team. A question can be asked and answered in seconds, without interrupting either person's flow of work. This means that errors and misunderstandings can be corrected promptly, and that knowledge is disseminated quickly. Junior developers can directly observe, copy, and learn from the more experienced members of the team.

You can keep abreast of the current situation by overhearing what your coworkers are saying to one another. Your neighbor can look over your shoulder, and help you fix problems with whatever is on your screen at the moment.

Even locating developers in offices along the same hallway is enough to break this effect. The action of standing up and moving away from your desk interrupts the flow of thought so much that most times you just won't bother, and when you do, it can take several minutes more to resume your previous level of concentration.

Physical proximity provides all the benefits of using the richest possible communications medium. People can discuss and directly see the impact of changes to a whiteboard diagram, and it's immediately apparent when someone is struggling with a problem, or when someone doesn't understand what you've just said.

Close/osmotic communication is an effective way to tackle the problem of communication overhead that we discussed in the context of time management's schedule development task. By spreading information around the team, you considerably reduce the need for ineffective and labor-intensive documentation. The cost of communication drops, and the team has greater flexibility. Everyone has the background knowledge required to work on any part of the system.

Alongside this requirement, and discussed elsewhere in the methodology, is the crossover between design and programming. There's no separation between the two roles: everyone is a "designer-programmer." In fact, given that there's rarely a dedicated tester on the team, the role is really that of "designer-programmer-tester."

4. Personal Safety

"Personal safety" is not physical safety, but rather the psychological and emotional safety needed to speak up freely without fear of censure or hostility. Problems like poor management decisions, a colleague's lack of attention to design, or even personal hygiene issues must be raised and resolved as soon as they become apparent.

Personal safety is an important adjunct to both close/osmotic communication and reflective improvement. If team members show trust and expose their ignorance by asking questions, then information can be efficiently transmitted to where it's needed. But if these questions are accompanied by ridicule, then the flow of questions and answers dries up rapidly.

Likewise, there's no point in organizing a reflection workshop if no one speaks up about the problems they're facing. The more confident people are that their comments and suggestions will be taken seriously, the more freely they'll offer them, and the better will be the information and ideas that are available to the team.

Some people show trust by default, whereas others only trust where they have seen positive evidence that trust is warranted. Gaining trust can be a slow process, so capable leaders will accelerate it by exposing themselves and their team to carefully chosen threats (for example, by revealing a weakness), and then showing that these lead to support, rather than hostility, and that there's no risk of being hurt.

Trust is enhanced by frequent delivery. When the results are on the wall for everyone to see, then people know who worked and who shirked, who spoke up and who kept quiet, who told the truth and who didn't, and who can be trusted and who can't. Peer pressure will ensure that team members remain trustworthy and dependable.

5. Focus

Crystal's "focus" property has two distinct meanings. The first is the ability to focus on an individual task in a single project for enough time to make effective progress. If the workday becomes fragmented, progress becomes increasingly difficult until project estimates become unachievable. The project can fail to meet its deadlines simply due to uncontrolled distractions.

The cost of switching context is high. Software is highly complex and highly abstract, and it takes considerable concentration to work effectively on it. This is often referred to as "flow." It may take 20 minutes to regain your train of thought after a phone call or a meeting, or more if it requires you to completely change tracks to discuss another project.

These interruptions are distinct from those experienced during close/osmotic communication. When you're working side by side with someone, you can tell if they're concentrating hard on something, and you can wait for them to take a break before asking your question. Also, a 30-second question won't disturb your concentration as much as a half-hour phone call or meeting.

Managers commonly assign developers to two or more projects at a time, but the consensus is that by the time the third project is added, the developer ceases to make effective progress on any of them. Management is a more piecemeal activity than development, and managers often fail to appreciate how much harder it is for developers to handle several areas of responsibility.

Crystal suggests two rules for dealing with these problems. The first is to define two-hour time windows when interruptions are blocked, because interruptions are rarely so critical that they can't be delayed for an hour or two. The second is to specify that when a person starts work on a project, they'll have at least two full days on that project before they can be asked to switch back again.

The second meaning of the focus property is related: it's the clarity and sense of direction the team needs to achieve its purpose successfully. Without a clear definition of your goals, how do you know if you're achieving them? The project's sponsor must ensure that the developers know what they're supposed to be working on by giving them an unambiguous mission statement. The developers must also be given clear and consistent priorities; they should be able to focus their efforts on one or two areas.

6. Easy Access to Expert Users

Even if most of the user requirements have been specified up front, these requirements should still be refined over the course of the project. The development team will work with an expert user to get feedback on the product, and to resolve any questions the developers may have.

It's important that this contact be a real user. Often the requirements are defined by a mid-level manager who has responsibility for the users, but who has never done their work and doesn't know how it is really done. A senior user or team leader would be more appropriate.

It would be ideal if that user could drop everything to join the project team, but expert users typically have too many responsibilities for this to be possible. A minimum level of involvement might be a weekly one- or two-hour meeting, plus availability for phone calls as required. This involvement could be adjusted to suit the project by means of reflective improvement.

A web-based application can be deployed to all the users at once by updates to a single server, but there are significant costs to deploying a desktop application to all the workstations. If the project team can't deliver the software to the entire user base frequently enough, then they can at least ask their expert user to trial each new version.

The developers can also train and work as users for a time. This is an unusual, and potentially expensive, strategy, but it may provide developers with a profound insight into the users' environment and issues.

7. Technical Environment with Automated Tests, Configuration Management, and Frequent Integration

Many traditional projects have an integration phase toward the end of the project. Typically, this is when the problems come to light. If the components have been developed separately, hundreds of subtle incompatibilities will exist between them. When the bugs become evident, there's no information as to which parts of the software are involved in the problem.

The ideal would be a development system that performs integration and testing on a continuous basis. If a developer checks in some changes that break the system, then these errors are identified immediately and can be located in the changes that have just been made. Errors have no chance to accumulate and overwhelm the project.

A system like this relies on three technologies. The first is configuration management, which "is steadily cited by teams as their most critical non-compiler tool" [Cockburn 2004]. It controls access to a master copy of the source code, and ensures that only one developer works on a particular part of the system at a time. All changes are recorded. This allows developers to work together, while protecting them from stepping on each other's toes. If problems are found, then changes can be reversed easily, and a specific configuration can be bundled up for release.

It takes significant time and effort to write the code for automated unit tests—the second technology—but developers often find that their overall productivity goes up when they do so. A number of explanations have been proposed:

- Automated testing takes less time than manual testing.

- The code is tested more frequently, so new bugs are found more rapidly.

- Unwanted changes to existing features can be easily found by running the accumulated unit tests for those features.

- The tests also serve as useful documentation for the requirements and functionality of the software.

- Test-driven development reduces the temptation to add flexibility and functionality that isn't required.

The third factor, frequent integration, is done by a *build process* that's scheduled to run on a regular basis. Microsoft established the idea of the overnight build, but in smaller software projects it may be feasible for the server to integrate and test the software several times a day. Developers can be notified of integration errors within minutes of the errors being introduced.

The software remains sufficiently bug-free so that it can be released at almost any time. Progress can be evaluated accurately, because there are no hidden integration and testing issues to provide unwelcome surprises further down the track.

Using Crystal

Crystal's strength is its flexibility. It can be slowly worked into an organization's existing processes without the disruption that normally accompanies significant change. Each of the properties can be progressively improved, quite independently of the others.

However, this flexibility makes it hard to know if you're "doing it right." The properties are fuzzy and easy to distort. For example, management may claim that they support the principle of personal safety and that anyone can speak freely, but staff members may just roll their eyes and say (to each other only) "Yeah, right."

Crystal is particularly appropriate for projects where

- The team has been together for a while.

- The developers are particularly adaptable and resourceful.

- It's a culture where professionals don't like being told how to do their work.

- The goal is to develop business software, rather than life-critical or real-time software (for example, aircraft control software).

Extreme Programming

Extreme Programming, commonly abbreviated to XP, is the enfant terrible of the industry. It's controversial, and deliberately so. It's the methodology that people have heard about, even if they know nothing else about agile software development. The word "extreme" is used to describe the way that "XP takes proven industry best practices and turns the knobs up to 'ten'" [Auer and Miller 2002]. XP includes 12 such practices:

1. The Planning Game	**7.** Continuous integration
2. Testing	**8.** On-site customer
3. Pair programming	**9.** Small releases
4. Refactoring	**10.** 40-hour week
5. Simple design	**11.** Coding standards
6. Collective code ownership	**12.** System metaphor

Critics decry XP as glorified hacking, but it actually requires considerable discipline to follow: more than Crystal, certainly. It insists that all of its 12 practices must be followed to fully realize its benefits. The methodology is presented as is, and there's no room in it for fine-tuning the process (Figure 5-2). This dogmatism is one of the reasons that people occasionally refer to Extreme Programming as a "cult." Another reason is its undeniable popularity among developers.

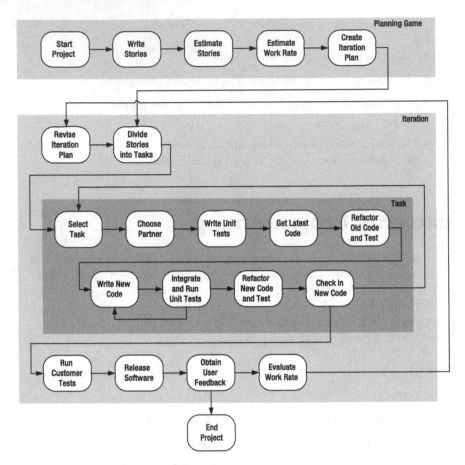

Figure 5-2. Unlike Crystal, XP's overall process can be represented in a flowchart.

I. The Planning Game

XP starts the development cycle by creating an iteration plan during the "Planning Game." The process is as follows:

- The customer concisely and plainly describes some behavior or functionality that they require in the software. This "story" is handwritten on a note card.

- Often, the customer also defines acceptance test criteria for the functionality, and writes them on the back of the card.

- The developer estimates the work required (in an arbitrary unit of measurement) and writes this on the same card.

- Depending on the resources available, and the experience from previous projects, the team members estimate how many units of work can be accomplished in each iteration (this is known as the "velocity").

- Each story should be small enough that a pair of developers can finish it within one iteration. If a story is too big, then it should be split up into several stories.

- The customer sorts the cards in the order that they'd like them to be completed, and divides them into piles. Each pile consists of a set of stories that the team can finish in one iteration.

These sets of features then become the plan for the project's series of iterations. The plan may be revised at the beginning of each iteration: the customer can reorder the cards if their priorities have changed. The developers can also revise their estimates, and the team's estimated work rate can be adjusted in view of the progress made during the previous iteration. The work is then broken down into individual tasks, and these tasks are assigned to specific developers.

This process quickly produces a rough plan, which can be refined on a regular basis as the situation becomes clearer. It also allows the customer to make the business decisions regarding which features should be implemented when, and gives them a sense of ownership and control over the project.

2. Testing

The rationale for automated testing is the same as for Crystal, but XP has added the requirement that the unit tests must be written before the code that is to be tested. This approach helps the developers to write only the minimum amount of code needed to run the tests successfully. The code has no unnecessary features, and it is as simple as it could possibly be. This avoids the risk of creating messy and confusing code.

The customer is also expected to create automated tests, but these will be acceptance tests to confirm that the software's features work the way they're supposed to. The project's progress can be measured by how many acceptance tests succeed at any given point in time.

However, the customer rarely has the development skills required to create these tests, so the developers will normally do the technical work for them. The customer will then just define the output data that they expect would be produced from some carefully chosen input data, and the developers will create a *test engine* that submits these inputs and checks the resulting outputs.

3. Pair Programming

Perhaps the most controversial aspect of XP is its insistence that every line of code must be created by a pair of developers sitting side by side. Developers change their partners daily. The benefits cited for this approach include

- Every line of code is reviewed for quality as it is written.
- Developers have an effective way to learn from one another.
- Knowledge about the software is spread throughout the team.
- The team can easily regroup if a developer gets sick or resigns.
- There is immediate social pressure to follow the team's conventions and rules.
- Brainstorming during design or debugging is more effective.
- The team develops cohesion and unity.

Managers are often initially skeptical, but research shows that while a pair is 15 percent less productive than two developers working alone, the resulting software has 15 percent fewer bugs and the overall cost is less [Cockburn and Williams 2000].

There are practical problems that must be overcome if this approach is to work. Often, the office layout must be reorganized to allow two developers to fit around each workstation: this usually means removing cubicle walls and throwing out those corner desks.

Also, developers commonly show resistance to pair programming. Many people are attracted to software development because they tend toward introversion, and enjoy the alone time that programming normally provides. Contrary to popular opinion, introverts are able to interact effectively with others, but they find it more tiring than working alone. There is a significant risk of burnout.

4. Refactoring

To *refactor* is to restructure existing code without changing its functionality in any way. The aim is to clean up and simplify the design, so that further progress can be made as rapidly as possible. The risk of introducing new defects will have been minimized.

One significant task is to remove duplicate code, which can be a major source of defects. Developers often borrow ideas from other parts of the code, so as not to reinvent the wheel. The problem is that when this code needs to be modified, there's no assurance that all of the copies will be found and updated. Human fallibility is allowed to creep in.

The solution is to bring together the common functionality into new routines and classes, thereby extending and enhancing the design. As the developers write the code, they learn what is needed in its design, and they continually revise the overall architecture.

XP suggests that refactoring should be done before new code is written, to prepare the design so that the new feature can be neatly integrated into the existing work, and "once and only once" [Auer and Miller 2002] to tidy up the code after it has been written. Automated testing means that you can refactor with confidence, because any bugs introduced during the process of refactoring will be spotted immediately.

5. Simple Design

"You're not going to need it" is the constant mantra of XP developers. There's tremendous pressure to simplify the design as much as possible and avoid unnecessary functionality. By aggressively managing the software's complexity, XP aims to maximize productivity and minimize the number of defects that appear. This improves extensibility because a simple design is easier to modify than a complex one.

Design has traditionally been done as an up-front activity. However, at this stage you don't know exactly how the software will work. Developers create designs that are as generic as possible, which can accommodate a wide range of possible implementations. But by doing so, they make the software more complex and more abstract than is necessary, which results in more work and more bugs.

With refactoring, the design can be adjusted constantly as the developers learn how best to implement the software. XP suggests that at any given point, you use the simplest design that can possibly work. This should

- Pass all of the automated tests created so far

- Contain no duplicate code

- Contain the fewest possible classes and methods

- Clearly state the programmers' intentions

The last point helps to address the common complaint that XP fails to provide documentation for completed software. Source code written during an XP project should be self-documenting. It should be clear enough that its intent is obvious to any future developer who works on it. The names of classes and methods should reflect their purpose, and avoid cryptic references and abbreviations.

6. Collective Code Ownership

All too often, responsibility for the code is divided among the developers, who "own" their own code and have little or no access to each other's code. This leads to a number of problems:

- Staff turnover can leave parts of the system without anyone who fully understands them, so no one can work effectively in those areas.

- There's less flexibility in assigning tasks to individual team members, so a developer may become a bottleneck during the project.

- The least experienced and least conscientious developers may create pockets of poor code that no one else is aware of.

- Integration between the areas of code is difficult, and work in one area may cause hidden problems in another.

In XP, everyone can make changes to any part of the system, so everyone is responsible for making sure that it works by running the complete set of automated tests. "You break it, you fix it" means that bugs are fixed, no matter what parts of the system they affect. A culture of fixing rather than finger pointing tends to bind the team together and bring a higher level of quality to the code.

An additional benefit is that developers acquire broad knowledge of how the whole system works, because they'll have worked on all of the parts themselves.

7. Continuous Integration

Just like Crystal, XP insists on a technical environment where the software under development can be automatically integrated and tested as often as possible. For XP, the primary goal is to sustain a rapid pace of development.

More traditional approaches tend to alternate between periods of coding and periods of debugging, which slows the overall rate of progress. Think of heavy traffic flow on a freeway: it can be either steady but slow, or stop-and-start. Stop-and-start introduces inefficiencies due to the frequent changes between braking and acceleration, so the overall traffic flow is slower.

Bug fixing is part of the daily development process in XP. Indeed, given that the tests are written first, the process is simply that of getting the tests to run successfully. Coding and bug fixing are effectively the same activity.

The advantage is that the code stays relatively free of bugs and remains a stable platform for further development. Bugs can be fixed individually, so there are fewer difficult situations where bugs obscure each other.

8. On-Site Customer

The Planning Game is just the start of the requirements-gathering process. The stories on the note cards aren't detailed enough to completely specify the features that they refer to. They serve instead as placeholders for features whose details will be fleshed out during development, in conversations between the developers and the customer. These requirements will be "documented" in the unit tests and the customer's acceptance tests.

This process requires that a customer representative be located alongside the developers throughout the project. For an internal project this isn't normally a problem, but an external client may find it difficult to find someone whose schedule is flexible enough.

The on-site customer representative makes critical business decisions about exactly how the software should work, and they will clarify priorities as to what features to develop first. But if they are junior enough that they can drop their other responsibilities to relocate to the developer site, then it's unlikely that they'll have the authority to make independent decisions that won't later be questioned or repudiated

Having a customer representative on-site allows issues to be dealt with very quickly, and the face-to-face discussions are the most effective way to convey information about the requirements.

9. Small Releases

XP's iterations always result in releasing a version of the software to the customer. The aim is to deliver real business value to the customer as soon as possible, so iterations should occur as frequently as possible while still introducing worthwhile functionality. The concrete feedback from each release can help to steer the progress of the next release.

This is a relatively inflexible approach. With typical iteration sizes of two to three weeks, the task of deploying the software can become a major overhead. Moreover, the customer may not want their operations to be disturbed every couple of weeks with yet more changes to their mission-critical software. They may prefer to coordinate their software deployment with user training and documentation activities.

10. 40-Hour Week

Tired is stupid. Unfortunately, because software is an especially complex and abstract product, it requires concentration to work with it effectively. Longer hours don't necessarily mean more progress.

"Those all-night programming stints make you feel like the greatest programmer in the world, but then you have to spend several weeks correcting the defects you installed during your blaze of glory," writes Steve McConnell [2004]. When there are many bugs, it may take longer to fix the software than it took to write it in the first place. The 40-hour week, like many of XP's practices, aims to improve both quality and productivity by avoiding such situations.

Another risk associated with ongoing overtime is that the developers use up the reserves they need to tackle any new problems, which might need to be resolved quickly. If you mess up, then you should work however long it takes to fix the problem, but this shouldn't happen on a regular basis. "If you burn the [midnight] oil long enough, sooner or later you run out of oil" [Auer and Miller 2002].

Overtime is often entrenched in a company's culture, and as a cost-free solution, it's often seen as the remedy of choice when a project fails to meet its deadlines. But because of its risks, overtime should be seen as a symptom of broader underlying problems in the project. Both the problems and the symptoms should be addressed.

11. Coding Standards

Coding standards ensure that the code is uniform in style and formatting. This boosts productivity by making the code easier to work with. It supports the XP practices by making it easier to refactor the code, easier to switch pairs, and easier to take collective ownership of the code.

Issues of style and formatting can create bitter disagreements between developers because they depend on personal preferences, and because there are no answers that are clearly better than others. They can develop into "religious wars."

It's better to defuse such issues before they arise by having the team agree up front to a set of coding standards. The standards need not be a rigid set of rules; they can be flexible guidelines that evolve over time as the team gains experience working together.

12. System Metaphor

A system "metaphor" isn't the same as a system's architecture, but it takes the same place in XP as an architecture does in other methodologies. In XP, the architecture develops over time as the code is written and refactored. The system metaphor provides a sense of direction to guide the development of the architecture; it doesn't dictate exactly what the system should look like when it is finished. The developers use the system metaphor to get a consistent picture of where new parts should fit, and roughly what they should look like.

One example of a system metaphor is the Model-View-Controller design pattern. It's often used to organize a program's code into distinct areas of responsibility:

- The Model contains all of the classes that define how the data is kept in memory, and it therefore serves as a representation of the business context.

- The View contains the classes that define the user interface. It provides a series of "windows" that present the data so that users can look at it and modify it.

- The Controller contains business logic that defines how the Model's data is updated and stored, and how the user navigates between screens or pages in the View.

Another example is the Publisher-Subscriber design pattern. One part of the system makes data available (i.e., it "publishes" the data), and then other parts of the system provide pathways through which they can receive that data (i.e., they "subscribe" to it). When new data becomes available, the Publisher sends copies of that data to all of its Subscribers.

The system metaphor encapsulates the understanding and vocabulary that the developers share. It will evolve over time, but it's useful to define something to start with. XP recommends that developers do not waste time finding the perfect metaphor, and that they should be prepared to abandon or supplement a metaphor if they find that it's of limited use.

XP also talks about the system metaphor as an aid to communication. The basic structure of the software should be comprehensible to the customer as well as to the developers, and a well-chosen metaphor can bring it to life.

Using XP

The biggest strength of XP is that its practices are clear and straightforward. They may not be easy to apply, but it's obvious whether they're being used or not. You can't disguise it if the developers refuse to work in pairs, or if no one is writing automated tests.

This clarity comes at the cost of limited flexibility. There's little guidance for those occasions when you need to adapt XP for specific circumstances. How can you implement pair programming if part of your team is offshore? How can you scale XP to work with very large projects? What do you do if your customer's decision makers can't or won't visit your site? XP has no answer for these questions. It was designed for a narrow range of project circumstances, and if your project doesn't fit into this range, then that's just too bad.

However, an active community has developed around XP, and many articles and papers have been written that attempt to address these (and other) concerns. Several new practices have been proposed to supplement the original 12, and there is now much more potential for modifying and fine-tuning XP than was originally intended.

XP is particularly appropriate for projects where

- The team has never worked together before.
- It's a culture where professionals expect to be told how to do their work.
- The customer and the developers work for the same company.
- The team doesn't contain any real introverts.
- The team is no larger than 10 or 12 developers.
- Speed of development is the most important issue.

The Rational Unified Process

Like both Crystal and Extreme Programming, the Rational Unified Process (RUP) was created in the late 1990s. Unlike both Crystal and Extreme Programming, though, RUP has a pedigree. It is a merger of the work of three of the leading lights in the field at the time: Grady Booch, Ivar Jacobson, and Jim Rumbaugh. In the mid-1990s, each of these experts had his own software development methodology, his own software modeling notation, and his own software company.

However, the uptake of these methodologies was slow because of the lack of standardization. To boost their revenues, they decided in 1995 to merge their methodologies, notations, and companies to create the Unified Process, the Unified Modeling Language, and the Rational Software Corporation ("Rational"), which was subsequently acquired by IBM in 2003. They themselves became known as the "Three Amigos."

RUP is Rational's version of the original Unified Process. RUP is widely used in commercial software development, and Rational claims that it "has emerged as a popular de facto standard modern software development process" [Larman et al. 2001]. It includes many of the innovations proposed by other agile methodologies, but retains a very different philosophy and flavor.

A RUP project consists of a sequence of iterations that's divided into four distinct phases: Inception, Elaboration, Construction, and Transition. The developers take on roles that define responsibilities for the activities within the nine workflows in RUP, and for creating the various RUP artifacts. Each of the phases, roles, activities, workflows, and artifacts is described in some detail, which makes RUP far more complicated than Crystal or Extreme Programming. This discussion will cover all of these topics, but in summary form only.

Despite the abundance of books and papers, there are a number of widely held misconceptions about RUP, whereas the truth is that

- The Rational Unified *Process* is not actually a process. It is instead a toolkit for building processes. All of the roles, activities, and artifacts are tools in that toolkit.

- Only very rarely would someone need every tool in the toolkit, and this would most likely be in the circumstances of a critical, multiyear project with hundreds of developers. Most teams can safely ignore most of RUP.

- You therefore can't really use RUP as-is out of the box. Before using it, you must first spend time on process configuration. This topic will be discussed later.

- "Rational Unified Process" is also the name of a software product available from Rational. The RUP software is relatively expensive, whereas you can get started with RUP, or with the original Unified Process, quite cheaply by buying a book or two. Project teams don't need to buy the RUP software to use RUP.

- A new version of RUP has appeared each year, and RUP has changed significantly over time.

- Rational produces powerful but complicated products, and RUP is no exception. It's hard to know how to get started; you can't just "add developers and mix well." There is no simplified version to get started with, and the full-scale RUP provides plenty of opportunities to shoot yourself in the foot.

- RUP is often described as an agile methodology, but it can be used in a very prescriptive, process-heavy way. The latter approach is more common for first-time users, particularly if they have neglected to perform process configuration. However, RUP can become an excellent agile methodology when correctly used [Larman 2002].

- RUP's four sequential phases appear similar to the discredited waterfall model. Naive users may use it in exactly this way, or they may try to disguise their existing flawed processes under RUP labels, but this isn't how RUP is intended to operate.

All too often, like the home exercise machines that so many of us purchase, RUP software is obtained solely for the feel-good factor. Managers who know that they need to do something about their development processes feel better for having made the financial commitment to RUP. However, without the personal commitment to use it properly, the product will provide no help whatsoever.

Phases

The waterfall model assigns a particular activity—such as requirements gathering or testing—to a specific phase of the project. In contrast, RUP's high-level activities, or "workflows," continue throughout the project (Figure 5-3).

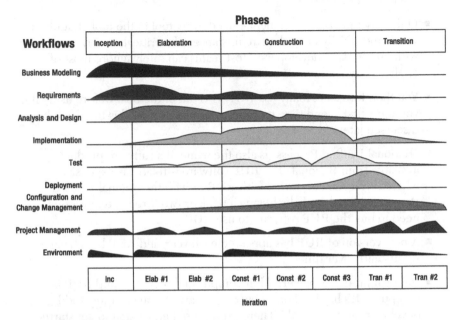

Figure 5-3. How RUP works in a typical project

The Inception phase is not just for gathering the requirements, nor is the Elaboration phase just for performing the analysis and design, nor is the Construction phase just for writing the code, nor is the Transition phase just for deploying the solution into production. This is a very common misconception.

Yes, the bulk of the requirements are obtained during the Inception and Elaboration phases, but this doesn't rule out updates to the requirements during the Construction phase.

The Inception phase is for defining the goals of the project. The overall scope is defined in broad terms, and enough of the architecture is worked out to ensure that a solution is possible. This phase also contains the project planning and start-up activities, as well as the initial process configuration for RUP.

During the Elaboration phase, the scope is refined by specifying the functionality and features of the proposed software in some detail. The overall architecture for the solution is developed to address these functional requirements. This architecture must also support service-level requirements such as performance and security. Alongside these activities, the developers put together a prototype to learn about and test any new tools and technologies.

The bulk of the effort goes into the Construction phase. Each iteration results in an additional portion of the functionality undergoing design, construction, and testing. The requirements may be adjusted as the customer has a chance to comment on the work so far. By the end of this phase, the software should be essentially complete.

In the Transition phase the software is progressively turned over to its users. This may include user acceptance testing, beta testing, and a phased deployment. New releases may be produced that fix any defects found during these stages. Documentation is finalized, and the users and support staff may be trained for the new system. The project team is disbanded at the end of this phase.

Iterations

Each phase can contain a number of iterations. This number isn't fixed, and Figure 5-3 shows just one example of how they can be organized. RUP recommends a total of three to nine iterations in the project. A duration from two to six weeks is suggested for the iterations, although iterations of up to eight months long are allowed for very large projects.

This is a different approach from Crystal and XP, which define the iteration size without regard to the total number of iterations in the project. They often have many more iterations during the course of their projects. RUP's smaller number of iterations means greater risk if any one iteration goes off course.

Roles

RUP currently defines at least 40 specific roles that team members can assume, including Architect, Code Reviewer, Database Designer, Technical Writer, and Use-Case Specifier. Each person in the project team takes responsibility for one or more roles, and each role may be performed by one or more individuals. The project manager decides which individuals take on which roles when she plans the project.

Artifacts

There are over a hundred distinct artifacts in RUP, and nearly all of them are documents or collections of documents. For example, the Software Development Plan includes a Risk Management Plan, a Product Acceptance Plan, and so on. Each artifact is created and updated by a specific role.

It's clearly overkill to produce all of these documents in every project. Unfortunately, RUP doesn't define a minimal set of artifacts that you can build on, and it's always more difficult to remove items from a list than it is to add them. RUP projects frequently demand more artifacts than are strictly necessary, which adds to the overhead and risk of these projects.

Interestingly, the Project Manager's artifacts are organized quite differently from those defined by the PMBOK (there's no Work Breakdown Schedule, for example), so a manager who wishes to use both RUP and the PMBOK faces a dilemma regarding which methodology to give priority to.

Activities and Workflows

The link between the artifact and the role is the activity. A role creates or updates an artifact as part of a specific activity. RUP's activities are far more closely defined than any we've seen so far. For example, RUP identifies six distinct activities just in the process of refining the architecture:

- Identify design mechanisms
- Identify design elements
- Incorporate existing design elements
- Describe runtime architecture
- Describe distribution
- Review the architecture

"Refine the architecture" is one of six "workflow details" in the Analysis and Design workflow. Within the nine workflows shown in Figure 5-3, RUP defines over 60 workflow details and hundreds of individual activities. Each activity is further broken down into a number of steps. The overall level of complexity is scary.

Process Configuration

The Environment workflow is where RUP defines the activities required to tune RUP for an individual project. The Process Engineer role creates the Development Case artifact, which is generally just a list of the artifacts to be produced during the project, with perhaps some notes about each one. Alongside this list there should be some guidelines for documentation, design, and programming.

"A process should not be followed blindly, generating useless work and producing artifacts that are of little added value. Instead, the process must be made as lean as possible . . ." [Kruchten 2000].

Apart from this assertion, RUP says little about how to select artifacts and activities, unlike Crystal, which gives specific guidelines for tuning the process according to the size of the project. No wonder first-time users struggle with RUP. The RUP software, though, provides a few predefined configurations for specific project types.

Use Case–Driven Development

The *use case* is perhaps RUP's most successful innovation: it's used far more widely than RUP itself. The use case is a technique for communicating requirements in a simple but structured and unambiguous way with customers, who may have no technical expertise whatsoever. For example, this use case defines what happens when a hotel guest uses their electronic key to open the door to their room:

Main flow:

1. The use case begins when the Guest inserts the key into the lock.

2. The system checks that the key is valid and, if so, unlocks the door.

3. The Guest removes the key and opens the door.

Alternative flow(s):

2a. If the key is not valid, a warning beep is sounded.

The use case defines a sequence of actions that ends up with a result that's of some value to whoever performs them. Defining the requirements in this way gives the developers enough detail to work with. All too often, customers ask for features rather than behaviors—"We need a search screen"—and fail to explain how they want them to work. Since the use case's result has value, it is also meaningful to the customer.

Use cases are a convenient way to group individual features. The collection of use cases defines the complete set of features that the system will have. Subsets of this group can be used to define the scope of individual iterations. The use case descriptions make it easy to do system testing: you simply perform each step in every use case. The use cases can also be converted into step-by-step user documentation.

Visual Modeling

Visual modeling is an important part of RUP. We've seen that the management of software complexity is one of the biggest challenges facing developers. A visual modeling language allows you to create a "map" for software that shows its structure in greater or lesser detail. By hiding details you can create a comprehensible overview of the system, and by exposing details you can show exactly how a small part of it works.

Many of RUP's artifacts are visual models. Visual models are used to depict the architecture and design of the software, and to communicate them to the development team. The quality of the architecture is easier to see in visual models, and by maintaining a good architecture, we ensure that the quality of the resulting software will be improved. As the software is modified, various tools can be used to keep visual models and code synchronized with each other.

Even though it comes from the same three contributors, the Unified Modeling Language (UML) is not part of RUP. In fact, RUP does not require that you use UML as the visual modeling notation, although virtually everyone who uses RUP does so. UML is not even a Rational product: it has been taken over as an industry standard by the Object Management Group.

Using RUP

In *How to Fail with the Rational Unified Process*, Larman et al. [2001] identify the following qualities as characteristic of a non-agile process:

- "Rigidity and control"

- "Many activities and artifacts are created in a bureaucratic atmosphere"

- "Lots of documents"

- "Elaborate long-term detailed planning"

- "Significant process overhead on top of essential work"

- "Process-oriented rather than people-oriented; treats people as pluggable parts in a mechanical method"

- "Predictive rather than adaptive"

It's easy to see how RUP can come to look like this. The development activities are described in painful detail, which can make the development process laborious and inflexible. There appears to be little scope for initiative, for looking around to see what needs to be done to make the project a success. And the whole concept of roles seems precisely designed to "treat people as pluggable parts."

It takes a lot of work to use RUP as an agile process. The work required to create a RUP configuration that suits small to medium-sized projects could easily become a project in itself. However, for large to very large projects, RUP comes into its own. A large project requires more documentation and greater formality in its development process. RUP includes enough structure and organization to allow software development on a scale that's simply not possible with XP.

Larman et al. [2001] compare RUP to a drug store; just because a vast range of drugs is available doesn't mean that you should take all of them for every ailment. However, in a drug store you'd leave the diagnosis and prescription to an expert, who would have a substantial body of reference material at hand. But RUP experts are few and far between, and there's little advice on how to apply RUP to individual situations.

Nevertheless, RUP encapsulates a great deal of knowledge that in other agile methodologies would come from the experience of the senior developers on the team. Developers can learn a lot from it, but they won't want do things by the book, nor should they be expected to do so.

RUP is particularly appropriate for projects where

- The team already has a suitable process configuration for RUP, or there's time to create a new one for the project.

- It's a culture where professionals expect to be told how to do their work.

- The team is very large.

- The goal is to develop life-critical or real-time software (for example, aircraft control software).

- Issues such as quality and reliability are more important than speed of development.

Mitigating Risks with Agility

When we discussed the PMBOK's approach to risk management, we outlined five specific risks that software development projects typically face. The agile methodologies' practices directly address these risks, and can be used to effectively mitigate them. This section analyzes specific XP and Crystal practices to find out which risks they mitigate. (RUP has been omitted from this analysis because, as we saw earlier, whether it is agile or non-agile depends on how it is used.)

The risks are discussed in the following sections.

1. Incomplete Requirements and Scope Changes

XP and Crystal use iterations to delay decisions on scope until just before the features are implemented, which limits the impact of scope changes. In XP, the on-site customer is intimately involved with the development process, and is consulted on every detail. Requirements are confirmed as the code is written, so any gaps in the requirements can be addressed as they become apparent. Crystal uses easy access to expert users to achieve the same end.

XP uses the Planning Game, and Crystal uses its focus property to allow the customer to define the priorities and schedule for the project in a flexible way. These strategies allow the inevitable changes in priorities to be accommodated without derailing the project.

2. Tools and Technologies Don't Work As Expected

The iterative approach also mitigates the risk of problems arising in the project's new tools and technologies. One common engineering approach to this problem is to first build a prototype that tests the new technology. Problems can be found at an early stage when there's still plenty of time to alter the product's design. The prototype is then thrown away.

In an iterative methodology, the product of the first few iterations is the prototype. You can test the new technologies on a small scale at an early stage, and you don't have to throw anything away. The prototype becomes the core of the new software. It can be refactored and improved as new functionality is added.

Up-front automated testing means that if something doesn't work, you find out about it quickly. There are no nasty surprises at the end of the project, when it's too late to do anything about it.

Crystal's personal safety property also allows the team to suggest and discuss any possible concerns at an early stage. Again, there's no need to wait until things go badly wrong before the issues are addressed.

3. Developers Lack Skills and Expertise

With XP's pair programming, developers have an effective way to learn from each other, and they can also monitor each other's expertise and progress. The equivalent principle in Crystal—close/osmotic communication—isn't as direct or as effective, but it has the same outcome.

The practice of simple design keeps the complexity of the software within the skill level of the whole team. Moreover, as the developers learn, they can go back and correct their earlier mistakes in design and coding through the process of refactoring. Crystal's reflective improvement also allows the developers to steadily improve their development process and environment.

4. The New Software Has Defects and Requires Rework

XP and Crystal use continuous integration and automated testing to ensure that the code remains free from defects. The tests are written alongside the code, so developers can feel confident that any new code is defect-free when it passes its unit tests. Rerunning previously written tests ensures that the existing code still works properly too.

Crystal's frequent delivery, which is the same as XP's small releases, ensures that the software is regularly cleaned up into versions that can be delivered to customers. There is a powerful incentive to sort out defect-ridden code, which might otherwise create ongoing problems in the system, before the customer sees it. Exposing the software to customer testing also helps the developers discover the limitations of their testing regime and find errors that wouldn't otherwise have come to light.

5. Project Staff Turnover

In pair programming, every piece of code is worked on by at least two developers, so there's always someone else who knows how something works. This reduces the risk if someone is "hit by a bus," i.e., changes to another project or to another job. Also, new developers can get up to speed quickly just by working side by side with an experienced team member

XP includes several techniques to make developers interchangeable, and to reduce the impact if someone does leave the team. Collective code ownership means that no code is off-limits, so everyone can and does make changes to code throughout the system. The use of coding standards gives the team a common format for their code, which makes it easier for people to work on each other's code. In addition, the system metaphor gives the team a common understanding of how the whole system fits together.

In Crystal, the corresponding property is close/osmotic communication, which allows the team to informally build a common understanding of the software under construction. Also, by reflective improvement, the team can agree on a common development environment and process, which may include standards for design and code.

For some developers, the agile methodologies can also improve job satisfaction and make it less likely that they will leave in the first place. These methodologies empower developers, and allow them to work more productively, with less frustration. The 40-hour workweek helps to avoid "death march" projects where developers burn themselves out and leave in droves.

Summary

Many of the agile practices improve software quality without affecting the course of the project, for example: automated testing, simple design, close/osmotic communication, and refactoring. They don't change how the project is managed, so they can be freely used in developing any piece of software.

Other agile practices, however, have a much bigger impact on the project. In particular, the use of iterations effects profound changes to the way that projects are run. In *How to Fail with the Rational Unified Process*, Larman et al. [2001] insist that "if an organization ... does not experience a deep and perhaps traumatic transformation at many levels in how they think about developing software, this is probably a sign that they didn't 'get' iterative development and truly adopt it."

These changes reduce the overall level of risk in projects, but they also make it hard to use practices from project management alongside practices from the agile methodologies. In the next chapter we will look at some techniques that can help to bridge the gap between the two.

But by making these changes, the agile methodologies avoid the invalid assumptions in project management that we identified in Chapter 3:

1. Scope can be completely defined.

2. Scope definition can be done before the project starts.

Agile methodologies don't require all of the scope to be defined up-front: scope definition is done throughout the course of the project.

3. Software development consists of distinctly different activities.

4. Software development activities can be sequenced.

5. Team members can be individually allocated to activities.

Agile methodologies treat development as a single activity, so design, coding, and testing are done concurrently. The developers are all doing the same job.

6. The size of the project team does not affect the development process.

Crystal defines explicit changes to the methodology depending upon the size of the project team. In XP, it's implicit that the methodology is intended for small teams or subteams of 2 to 12 developers.

7. There is always a way to produce meaningful estimates.

8. Acceptably accurate estimates can be obtained.

9. One developer is equivalent to another.

Estimates can be based on the experience of prior iterations, which allows you to build up a history of real metrics to make estimation more accurate. You don't need to guess how much work an arbitrary developer can get done, because you know exactly how productive your particular team has been.

10. Metrics are sufficient to assess the quality of software.

The developers continually review each other's code to assess its quality and find problems. In XP, the relevant practices are pair programming and collective code ownership. In Crystal, it's close/osmotic communication and reflective improvement.

Budgeting Agile Projects

In the previous chapter, we saw how agile methodologies can help developers avoid the invalid assumptions in project management that we identified in Chapter 3. The main goal the agile methodologies address is how to efficiently create high-quality software that meets the customer's needs. Anything that has been found to contribute to this goal has been included in one or more of the methodologies. Anything that doesn't contribute to it has been left out.

Efficiently creating high-quality software gets us a long way toward having a successful software project, so it makes sense to use an agile methodology. But there's one big drawback: by allowing ongoing scope definition, the agile methodologies make it hard to fix a project's budget. How can we ensure that our project will be profitable if we don't know how much it will cost? If we can find ways to address this issue, then we'll be able to complete our solution (started in the previous chapter) for the problems outlined in Part One.

In this chapter, we'll start by discussing the issues around the budgeting of software development projects. We'll then introduce seven techniques that can be used alongside the agile methodologies to make their estimation processes more accurate, and to make it easier for them to stay within a fixed deadline and budget:

1. Continuous development

2. On-demand programming

3. SWAT teams

4. Subteam encapsulation

5. Feature trade-off

6. Triage

7. Scoping studies

Each technique can be used individually, but they can also be used together. After discussing each technique in turn, we'll consider how best to combine them for different types of software projects. Finally, we'll take a brief look at the controversial subject of offshore outsourcing, to see whether it really can deliver its promised cost benefits, and whether it can be done in an agile way.

In the next chapter, we'll see these techniques in action as we rework the case study from Chapter 4 to show how it could have succeeded had the project been managed differently.

Budgeting for Software Development

By using practices from the agile methodologies, we can mitigate the most common software development risks and ensure that we create software that works well and meets the customer's needs. However, this doesn't guarantee that the development can be done within a particular deadline or budget. In fact, by spreading out the scope definition process over the course of the project, it can be more challenging to create a budget for the software development as a whole. As the scope is changed during the course of the project, so too are the estimates for cost and duration. The agile scope definition process bypasses the mechanisms that the PMBOK uses to control scope changes.

If the customer is allowed to think up too many changes and new features, then the software may never be finished. This isn't as bad as it seems, because frequent delivery ensures that the customer quickly benefits from any new development work. The agile practices stop uncontrolled change holding back the software from being deployed. They also protect the quality of the software through all the changes, but they don't stop it from blowing out the budget.

Here we encounter the critical difference between commercial and non-commercial software. Noncommercial software doesn't have a budget, and isn't limited by cost, so it's OK to use as many developer hours as it takes to get it right. That's how open source development projects are run, and that's one of the reasons why they're so successful in producing high-quality software.

However, commercial software development is undertaken for the sole purpose of getting a good return on the money invested in developing the software, either by making money or (more often) by saving money in streamlining a company's operations. Compromises must be made to find the functionality that provides "the biggest bang for the buck." That's why it's so important for customers to know exactly how much they must pay for the software before they commission it.

During the late 1990s dot-com era, it might have been acceptable to engage in ongoing speculative development in the hope that an initial public offering (IPO) for the fledgling company would reap billions from the stock market, but those days are gone for good. Nowadays a project won't go ahead unless the return on the investment is good enough.

"We start with payback period," says Ron Fijalkowski, CIO at Strategic Distribution Inc. in Bensalem, Pennsylvania. "For sure, if the payback period is over 36 months, it's not going to get approved. But our rule of thumb is we'd like to see 24 months. And if it's close to 12, it's probably a no-brainer" [Anthes 2003].

To meet these requirements, a new piece of software must enhance revenue or save costs equivalent to its development budget during the first two years in production (see Figure 6-1). IT systems go out-of-date very quickly, so it makes sense to evaluate them on the basis of time. Even if technology changes so fast that you have to replace your new system within three years, with a payback period of two years you're still ahead.

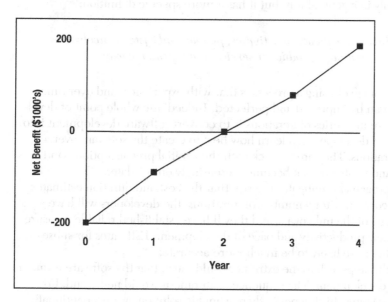

Figure 6-1. The return on investment for a project with a two-year payback period

A payback period calculation requires an accurate estimate of the development costs for a new piece of software. In these circumstances, it's no longer acceptable to allow development costs to vary uncontrollably during the course of a project. We must find ways to constrain the cost that don't conflict with the agile practices, and that still allow developers to create software of acceptable quality. Moreover, we have an additional risk to mitigate: the cost and duration estimates might be incorrect.

1. Continuous Development

If it's too difficult to provide reliable estimates for software development in the context of projects, then there's an obvious solution: don't create your software in projects.

This isn't as irrational as it sounds. A project is "a temporary endeavor undertaken to create a unique product or service" [PMI 2000]. However, when developers write software, each feature that they add has similarities to the ones that come before and after it. They're similar in that they're all features of the same piece of software. The software may be unique, but the features are not. The development team can become a production line that adds one feature after another to the software under construction.

We use a *project* to create a unique product or service, and we use a *process* to create a nonunique product or service. We've so far used the word "process" only in a general way, but it has a more specific definition:

> *A process is a sequence of activities, people, and systems involved in creating a product or service in a repeatable way.*

The advantage of using a process is that with experience, and over time, the process can be improved and perfected. Indeed, the whole point of developing software in a series of iterations is to convert software development into a process. The developers can learn how best to create the software over a series of iterations. They aren't stuck with their initial preconceptions, and with plans and strategies that become increasingly out-of-date.

This approach also mitigates the risk that the cost and duration estimates might be incorrect. After a number of iterations, the developers will have resolved many of the unknowns, and they'll have established reliable measurements for their productivity and pace of development. Estimates for subsequent iterations are likely to be much more accurate.

Taking this approach to the extreme would mean that the software is under continuous development. The sequence of iterations would never end. For many large systems this is a perfectly reasonable solution, as they continually accumulate a backlog of change requests.

Eric Raymond [2000b] writes that "there is empirical evidence that approximately 95% of code is still written in-house. This code includes most of the stuff of [the IT department], the financial- and database-software customizations every medium and large company needs. . . . Most such in-house code is integrated with its environment in ways that make reusing or copying it very difficult. . . . Thus, as the environment changes, work is continually needed to keep the software in step. This is called 'maintenance,' and any software engineer or systems analyst will tell you that it makes up the vast majority (more than 75%) of what programmers get paid to do."

Managers can obtain accurate estimates for the cost of each change, and they can prioritize and approve individual pieces of work from iteration to iteration. Unfortunately, it's very difficult to evaluate the cost savings from such small changes, so it isn't practical to do a payback period calculation for each one. A better approach is to decide how much the software is worth to the organization on an ongoing basis, and then fund the development team accordingly.

Maintenance is generally done by in-house software development teams, as there's less overhead and the organization can maintain a team of developers with exactly the right skills and areas of expertise. The developers are on hand to resolve problems, help users, and look after the production environment. However, there's less flexibility to significantly increase or decrease the pace of development. If you can't redeploy developers from one team to another, then the only option is to hire and fire—which isn't always straightforward.

2. On-Demand Programming

Organizations are increasingly frustrated by the lack of flexibility in their IT systems in view of how much they have invested in them. The problem is that system usage varies through the day, and also in weekly, monthly, and yearly cycles. A system that's only designed to handle average levels of load would grind to a halt at times of peak load, but a system that's designed to handle the peak load would have ample spare capacity sitting idle most of the time.

There is a new IT industry trend to supply computing power as though it were any other utility. After all, why buy a power station when you can draw electricity from the grid? On-demand computing lets customers avoid big up-front purchases of computer hardware, and gives them the ability to handle unforeseen surges in demand. Setting up the connection to the system takes some work, but subsequently a single contract for the supply of services covers circumstances that can vary as required.

"IBM's on-demand server hosting services are designed to let customers add or subtract computing power and pay monthly only for what they use. IBM estimates that companies using its hosted services will spend 30% less on IT operations than if they ran comparable systems themselves," reports Larry Greenemeier in *InformationWeek*.

Why not do exactly the same thing with software development?

We saw that an in-house team of developers limits the flexibility of an organization to increase or decrease the pace of development for its mission-critical software. New initiatives come at irregular intervals and involve large surges in workload, which disrupts the stability needed to make continuous development operate smoothly. But scheduling each initiative as a one-off project carries with it its own set of risks, which we've already discussed in detail.

On-demand programming is an extension of continuous development, but it's more flexible. The supplier maintains a team of developers that know how to work on the customer's systems, but they don't work on them all the time. The developers are hired only when they're needed, and at other times they work for other customers. There's still an endless series of iterations, but there may be gaps between groups of iterations.

Over the course of a year, for example, an on-demand team could divide their time into fortnightly iterations for three different customers (see Figure 6-2).

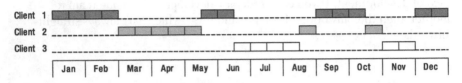

Figure 6-2. A year's work for a typical on-demand team

This is not the same as taking individual developers out of a pool to assign them to isolated projects. The critical factor is the experience the team gains by working on a particular system. This allows them to estimate new work far more accurately than would otherwise be possible.

Unlike project-based development, only a single ongoing contract exists between customer and supplier. The customer only pays for the developer time that they actually use. However, this approach works best when there's a strong relationship between the two parties, and where the customer trusts the developers to deliver their "best effort" in the time available. An exhaustive and rigid contract is not helpful.

Problems can occur in scheduling work from different customers so that individual assignments don't conflict with one another. Servers can be loaded with new software very quickly, but developers take time to develop expertise with a particular system, which makes it hard to swap teams within an engagement.

3. SWAT Teams

On-demand programming requires adaptable, general-purpose teams that have the expertise to work on systems for several different customers. These teams can hit the ground running, not only for customers and systems that they have already worked with, but also for customers and systems that are unfamiliar to them, or even to build new software from scratch.

The SWAT team model is based on military or police SWAT teams. The purpose of the Special Weapons and Tactics (SWAT) team is to provide emergency tactical response to life-threatening incidents. The SWAT team is able to respond quickly and effectively because they have already worked out their operational strategies and tactics, and because they have trained and worked together. They know how to get the most from their team. No time is wasted getting themselves set up and sorted out. Team members know and trust one another, and their shared experience gives them confidence in their skills, and confidence that they can achieve the right outcome no matter what situation they find themselves in.

A software development SWAT team would have a range of skills that could include

- Software design and architecture

- User interfaces and usability

- Databases and data storage/retrieval

- Hardware and network infrastructure

- Client liaison and user training

The developers would still do the same job—we've seen how dividing work by specialization can lead to problems—but each person would bring their own expertise to the team. This creates a well-rounded team that can be used for a wide range of problems.

Developer skills don't need to be technology specific: you'll need a database expert in the team, for example, rather than an expert on Oracle database software. Detailed technical knowledge for particular products can be obtained by research and by problem solving on the job, so what's needed is deep familiarity with the underlying concepts in a specific area of technology.

This is particularly true for the enterprise application frameworks, the toolkits that are used to build modern software systems. Over the last few years there has been a move away from proprietary technologies and toward common standards. There are now only two major enterprise application frameworks: Java 2 Enterprise Edition (J2EE) from Sun, IBM, BEA, etc. and Microsoft's .NET.

But writing code in C# for .NET is little different from writing code in Java for J2EE. The two technologies use the same underlying concepts, and have more similarities than differences. It's easy to apply skills from one to the other. An experienced team should be able to handle tasks in either area, which means they can develop virtually any significant new software, no matter what technology is used.

The advantage of using a SWAT team is that they'll have established and perfected their own development process, and can apply it to a wide range of tasks. Using a team with a proven track record is less risky than creating a new team from scratch. The team's history and metrics will improve the accuracy of their estimates for any new software development work.

4. Subteam Encapsulation

Agile methodologies rely on frequent, face-to-face communication between the members of a software development team. As the team grows larger, this becomes more and more difficult. The number of communication paths in a team increases much faster than the size of the team (see Figure 6-3).

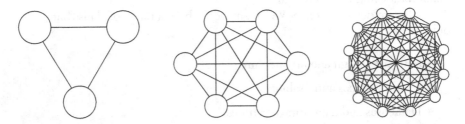

Figure 6-3. Communication paths in teams with 3, 6, and 12 members

   Agile software development works best with small teams of two to ten developers who sit together, and who can easily talk to each other whenever they need to. But not every project can be tackled by a small SWAT team. What do you do if there's more work than ten developers can accomplish within a reasonable time frame? How do you manage the complexity of a large team while still keeping the benefits of agile development?

   Let's look at other complex systems to see how their complexity is managed. The most complex systems arise in software development, and computer scientists have invented several techniques to simplify them. One of the most promising is encapsulation. In Chapter 2, we saw how it could be used to make a complex system much simpler (see Figure 6-4). Why not apply this technique to the organization of a software development team?

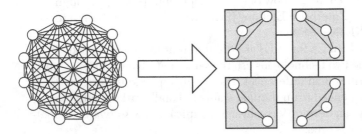

Figure 6-4. Encapsulation can simplify a complex system.

The key features of encapsulation are:

1. The system is divided into smaller components.

2. The internal complexity of these components is hidden behind a simple interface.

3. Components communicate with each other whenever they need to.

4. All communication is peer-to-peer; there is no hierarchy.

5. Each component has its own specific responsibilities.

Applying this technique to the organization of a team means that:

1. The team is divided into smaller subteams.

2. A subteam doesn't need to know how another subteam organizes itself. They always talk to the same member of that subteam. We can call this person the "mediator."

3. A mediator is always available. They should be as accessible as any other member of a subteam. This means that each mediator is a member of two or more subteams.

4. A mediator is not a leader. They serve as a conduit for information; they don't tell their colleagues what to do. Information does not travel up and down some kind of hierarchy, but horizontally—between equals.

5. Each subteam has well-defined areas of responsibility, which overlap other subteams' responsibilities as little as possible.

Figure 6-5 shows how a team of 15 developers can be divided into three subteams of six developers. Each pair of subteams has a mediator (highlighted) who is a member of both subteams. Each subteam has 15 communication paths, so there are 45 communication paths in total. This is the same number of communication paths as an undivided team of 10 developers (see Figure 6-5). In this example, encapsulation allows us to increase the size of a team by 50 percent without adding to the communication overhead.

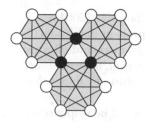 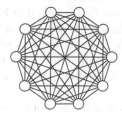

Figure 6-5. A team of 15 can be just as agile as a team of 10.

5. Feature Trade-off

Even the best estimates from an experienced SWAT team will be of no use if the customer adds feature after feature to the software during development. Allowing the customer to refine the requirements during the course of a project is an important part of any agile methodology. But customers often want to fix the development period to ensure that the cost remains within their budget by, for example, booking the development team for a specific number of iterations.

The simplest solution is to allow the customer to change their mind and specify new features, but only if they let go of other features at the same time. One feature is traded off against another. Features can often be implemented in a variety of ways; some allow more flexibility but are more complex, whereas others are simpler and more straightforward. If necessary, the developers can suggest ways to modify the requirements that allow the software to remain within its original budget.

There are potential interpersonal issues here. The customer will want to retain control over the requirements and scope, and naturally so; they pay the bills, after all. However, if they want to change the scope while keeping the budget the same, then something has to give. If the customer wants flexibility, then they'll have to show flexibility.

6. Triage

Stedman's Medical Dictionary defines triage as

> *A process for sorting injured people into groups based on their need for or likely benefit from immediate medical treatment. Triage is used in hospital emergency rooms, on battlefields, and at disaster sites when limited medical resources must be allocated.*

Although triage was originally a medical term, it now has a broader meaning, which is to allocate any scarce commodity—such as developer time—to the areas where you can derive the most benefit from it.

The concept of triage was first outlined in Edward Yourdon's [2004a] famous book *Death March*, but triage is also useful for projects that haven't yet become a death march. Triage is a way to prioritize development effort, so the best use can be made of limited developer time. However, instead of sorting people by their medical condition, developers sort features by their value to the customer.

The 80/20 rule tells us that 20 percent of the features will be responsible for 80 percent of the benefits in any piece of software. This is confirmed by Standish Group [2001] research, which shows that on average only 20 percent of software features in existing applications are "always" or "often" used, and that 45 percent of features are never used (see Figure 6-6). The key is to identify that 20 percent, so you can ensure that it's completed no matter what else happens in the project. This is the minimum marketable feature set: the minimum amount of functionality that will deliver the maximum amount of value.

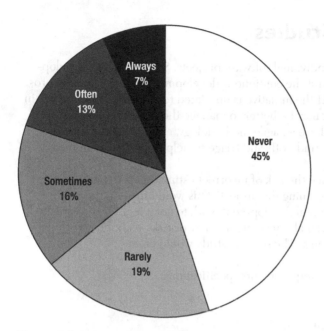

Figure 6-6. Software feature usage

Yourdon [2004a] suggests asking the customer to divide the software's features into three groups: "must-do," "should-do," and "could-do." The must-do group will be completed first, then the should-do group and finally the could-do group. Within a group, the highest risk features are tackled first. These groups should be evenly balanced. If the customer can't or won't prioritize the features in this way, then this is itself a sign of underlying problems.

This strategy reduces the impact of any risks in the project, particularly with regard to incorrect estimation, because if the software can't be completed in the time allowed, then the missing features will be those that have the lowest value for the customer.

Also, if the customer changes their mind and proposes drastic changes to the scope during the course of the project, then the developers will have a list of low-value features that can be traded off against the new features that the customer wants.

If the project encounters any significant problems, triage can be useful in drawing attention to the real priorities. In these circumstances, developers must focus their efforts on getting the project back on the rails. Any attempt to make up lost ground will only drag the project down even further.

"When you're in project-recovery mode, it's easy to focus on the wrong issue: how to finish *quickly*, how to *catch up*? This is rarely the real problem. For projects that are in this much trouble, the primary problem is usually how to finish *at all*" [McConnell 1996].

7. Scoping Studies

There's still a place for individual software projects. Some software development work just doesn't suit the continuous development and on-demand programming approaches. If the initiative is unrelated to any other recent work in the organization, then it may be better to manage the work as a stand-alone project. But you can still use an agile methodology, employ a SWAT team, and make use of feature trade-offs and triage to help the project run more smoothly.

Another way to reduce the risk of incorrect estimation is to perform a scoping study before beginning the project. This would firm up the requirements and include some real development work to get a feel for the expected level of productivity. It can also test out any new or risky technologies to uncover potential problems. The scoping study would create

- Use cases or other requirements specifications
- Screen mock-ups
- A high-level design
- Working code for a few key features, with unit tests
- An acceptance test plan
- A breakdown of the work, with estimates
- An iteration plan

The scoping study should be organized and funded as a separate project in itself, not as part of the main project—although it would be equivalent to the RUP Elaboration phase for that project. It provides the information needed to effectively plan the main project, which is why it must finish before the project starts. You can evaluate the project with much better information, but you must be prepared to walk away from the money expended on the scoping study if the study shows that the main project is not viable. Be prepared to allocate 10 percent to 20 percent of your overall budget to the scoping study.

A scoping study can be particularly effective when the work is performed by an external contractor. External contractors are often forced to skimp on the project planning process because they need to minimize their outlay, and hence their exposure, before the contract is signed. The risks that accrue from this are mitigated by sizable contingency costs, particularly in fixed-price contracts. However, if the customer pays the contractor to perform a proper requirements gathering and project planning phase—i.e., a scoping study—then the overall cost will be lower since they won't be paying the contractor to assume as much risk.

The goal of the scoping study is to build a mock-up of the proposed new software that gives the customer and the users a real feel for how the whole thing will work. In a modern development environment, it's easy to create static screens filled with sample data that look exactly like the proposed application. For a web application, the web pages would be written by hand, and there would be no code to generate them automatically. They'd include fixed hyperlinks to navigate from one page to another.

Unlike an ordinary mock-up, though, these screens don't have to be thrown away. They can form the foundation of the real application as its logic is built up feature by feature. Building the mock-up contributes real progress to the project; it's not an overhead. The same applies to the key features developed during the scoping study.

The same team should be used for the scoping study as for the main project; otherwise the metrics obtained from this exercise are of little value. The team also benefits from the experience they gain with the system during the course of the scoping study.

If having two separate contracts proves awkward, an alternative approach is to conduct a scope review partway through the project. The scope review follows a scoping study phase, as described previously, which allows the initial ballpark estimates to be revised and reevaluated. The client can cancel or trim down the project if it turns out to be too expensive.

Combining These Techniques

To show how combinations of these techniques can be used for different kinds of software development situations, we'll consider four major categories of software projects. The categories are divided according to whether it's a major system or a minor application, and whether the work is for existing, legacy software or whether it's a proposal for a new piece of software (see Table 6-1).

Table 6-1. Many Techniques Are Useful Only for Specific Types of Software Projects

Technique	Major Legacy System	Minor Legacy Application	Major New System	Minor New Application
1. Continuous development	✔			
2. On-demand programming		✔		
3. SWAT teams		✔		✔
4. Subteam encapsulation			✔	
5. Feature trade-off		✔	✔	✔
6. Triage	✔	✔	✔	✔
7. Scoping studies			✔	✔

Major Legacy System

An organization's major legacy systems are likely to be mission-critical for them, so it makes sense to develop them in-house. This ensures security of supply. The organization won't be affected if their outsourcing provider goes bust, and they can't be held hostage by their suppliers through "vendor lock-in."

A major legacy system will generate enough user problems, change requests, and ongoing issues to support continuous development. Starting up and shutting down projects for all of these tasks would add an enormous amount of overhead, so it's better to perform the work as an ongoing series of iterations. A general-purpose SWAT team is not required; the team members only need the specific skills required for this system.

Triage is essential. The team will receive a wide range of requests, of which only a small fraction would actually provide some tangible benefit to the organization. These requests must be prioritized in some way. But feature trade-off is less critical, because important issues will eventually be addressed— if not in the current iteration, then in a subsequent one.

Minor Legacy Application

Minor applications demand much less work than major systems, and are less likely to be critical, so it would be wasteful to have dedicated personnel. It makes more sense to organize a SWAT team that can work on a wide range of applications. An organization can maintain its own development team, or it can select an outsourcing provider to provide on-demand programming services. Requests accumulate until there is enough work for an iteration, or a short series of iterations, to clear the backlog.

Triage is just as important as for major legacy systems. Requests must be prioritized, because only a small fraction of the work is really worth doing. The work rate is hard to estimate, because less work has been done on the application over its lifetime, so there has to be some flexibility in the plan of work. Depending on the work rate that the team manages to achieve, they may have to shed tasks to meet their deadline, or they may be able to complete more tasks than expected.

Feature trade-off is also important: there must be some way to accommodate urgent requests. If an important feature or bug fix doesn't make it into the current plan of work, then it's likely to be quite some time before the application is worked on again.

Major New System

Offshore outsourcing begins to make sense for the amount of work required to develop a major new system. The potential financial benefits may compensate for the additional hassle and overheads (discussed in the next section). However, it might be helpful to hire a few key people on a permanent basis to provide continuity beyond the end of the project. They can form the core of the team that will support the system once it goes into production, when it becomes a legacy system.

A big project is a big risk, and a separate scoping study project can help reduce that risk. Because of the size of the project, the overhead of having two (or more) contracts is manageable. A SWAT team can help get the scoping study off the ground quickly, but for the main project the team will be together long enough that it makes sense to build it around the specific skills required for the project. Because it's likely to be a large team, the technique of subteam encapsulation can help the team work together more efficiently and effectively.

Triage is critical. A large project is extremely difficult to estimate with any degree of accuracy, because there are so many interrelationships. A problem in one area can lead to problems in other areas, which may in turn lead to still more problems, and so on. Triage helps to prioritize issues, so that many of them can be dismissed before they spiral out of control.

It's hard to gauge day-to-day progress on a long project, and it's easy to accumulate one small slip after another, until the deadline becomes hopelessly unachievable. With triage, small slips can be immediately compensated for with corresponding adjustments to the overall scope of the project.

A long project allows people plenty of time to change their minds or think up new ideas. Indeed, over a period of months or years, many of the individuals who originally developed the requirements may have left the organization, to be replaced by new people who have different priorities. Without feature trade-off, this can result in a never-ending series of additions and changes to the requirements.

Minor New Application

Finally, with a small-scale project there's less potential benefit to set against the overheads of offshore outsourcing. However, the project would still create a surge in workload for an in-house development team, so in many cases a local outsourcing provider will be the best choice. They should provide a flexible, multi-talented SWAT team that can quickly adapt to the specific requirements of the project.

The overhead of a separate scoping study *project* is probably not justified, but a scope review after an initial scoping study *phase* would be useful to gauge progress, firm up requirements, and allow for mid-course corrections.

While triage and feature trade-off are not as critical as for a major project, a minor software project can still benefit from them. They can help to ensure that the project sticks to its original budget and deadline.

The next chapter describes a case study that explores these techniques in more detail, in the context of a project to develop a minor new application.

Agile Offshore Outsourcing

To finish up, let's take a brief look at the controversial subject of offshore outsourcing, to see whether we can use agile techniques to help an offshore project succeed. Offshore outsourcing may be the only way to make a project profitable if its budget is really tight, but this is not a decision to be taken lightly.

We've seen that one of the biggest challenges in software development is making person-to-person communication as effective as possible. The best way to keep your customers, users, managers, and developers talking to each other is to locate them as close together as possible. But if your company has outsourced its development work to Bangalore or Beijing, while keeping its managers and users in Boston or Berlin, then this is likely to cause significant problems. Offshore outsourcing adds considerable risk to software development, so you should avoid it if you can.

Increasingly, though, executives are attracted by the potential cost savings from employing people in countries where the local salaries are five to ten times lower. Executives often have limited awareness of the issues around software development, and presume that they can just send over a requirements document and then wait for the completed software. This approach doesn't work very well.

Salon.com reports that "For [Celeste] Smith, who would love nothing better than to hire back her U.S. programmers, the dot-com run-up and the current mania for [offshore] outsourced labor share an eerie similarity. In both cases, she says, top-level managers have valued the actions of competitors and investors higher than the actual information coming back from the marketplace.

'I've talked to a few people in my position,' she says. 'In general, when senior management makes a decision to outsource [offshore], there's political pressure to pretend it's working just so they don't look stupid. That's happening here, too' " [Williams 2004].

Offshore outsourcing can succeed, and it can make an otherwise unpromising project possible by significantly reducing its costs, but it takes a lot of work to get it there. The same risks apply as for any other project, but to a much greater degree. Communication is difficult when you're on the other side of the world from your development team. You must work that much harder at communication, and indeed at all of the agile best practices. Some helpful hints:

- Ensure that *all* of the developers speak your language fluently.

- Invest in good videoconferencing tools.

- Don't let the difference in time zones be a factor. Ask the development team to change their hours so that they're at work when you're at work. You'll want to be able to resolve issues instantly. You shouldn't have to wait 24 hours to get a decision or a clarification.

- Send over at least one person who can make instant business decisions: the on-site customer is no longer an option—it's a necessity.

- For geographically distributed teams, try organizing the team into encapsulated sub-teams. Ask the mediators to commute between the subteams' locations.

- Invest in just as much training for your offshore developers, if not more. Remember, they probably can't afford the best books, courses, and certifications on the salary that you'll be paying them.

- Arrange to deliver the software frequently, to confirm progress and check quality.

- People from Asian cultures are often more polite than Westerners, and hence less outspoken and blunt. Your team leader should have deep experience of the team's culture, so they can be aware of any problems as soon as possible. This is less of a problem when outsourcing to western nations.

- Pay attention to the corporate culture. Effective use of an agile methodology requires a degree of flexibility and individual empowerment that may be difficult to achieve in certain cultures.

- Before you risk millions of dollars with a large mission-critical project, try it out first with a small pilot project to see how well it works for you, and where the problems are. Does it actually generate the level of savings that you expected?

Summary

In the previous chapter, we discovered that the agile methodologies can form part of a solution to the problems in software development projects. But they're not the whole solution. They can help us successfully create software, but they can't ensure that our projects will be profitable. In this chapter, we've introduced seven further techniques that can help make the estimation process more accurate, and make it easier to stick to a fixed deadline and budget:

1. **Continuous development:** Turn software development into a continuous process that has a fixed operating cost.

2. **On-demand programming:** Use the same team for ongoing work on several systems to make their projects more efficient and predictable.

3. **SWAT teams:** Keep your team together, so you can use data from previous projects to help estimate future ones.

4. **Subteam encapsulation:** Link up several small teams peer-to-peer to make large projects as efficient as small ones.

5. **Feature trade-off:** Keep the total workload constant by eliminating tasks whenever new ones are added.

6. **Triage:** Maximize the value of software created within a fixed budget by prioritizing the work.

7. **Scoping studies:** Reestimate the project when part of it has been completed to make the estimates more accurate.

Case Study: The Billing System Revisited

In the previous two chapters we've looked at a series of techniques that can help to solve the problems outlined in Part One. In Chapter 5 we saw techniques that can resolve the issues around software quality. In Chapter 6 we saw techniques that can constrain an agile project to a fixed deadline and budget.

In this chapter we'll look at the same techniques from a different perspective. We'll use another case study—one that addresses the same business initiative as the case study described in Chapter 4—to show how these techniques can be combined to produce a complete solution for the problems in software project management, and how our suggested approach can lead to a more successful outcome. At the end of the chapter we'll see how the new techniques helped the project team avoid the invalid assumptions that we identified in Chapter 3. This is where our journey ends.

Methodology

The case study is a project to create a new, relatively small piece of software, so we'll see the following techniques from Chapter 6 in action:

- SWAT teams
- Feature trade-off
- Triage
- Scoping studies

The team will employ techniques from two agile methodologies. A high-level structure of phases and iterations from the Rational Unified Process will be supplemented with lower-level practices from Extreme Programming. This is an unusual but perfectly valid approach. We'll be focusing on the interactions between the members of the team, so only the following practices will feature in our discussion:

- **Testing:** Manual acceptance test scripts will be used alongside the automated unit tests, because in this case it's less expensive than creating or purchasing a test engine for them.

- **Pair programming:** The developers will switch partners at the end of each iteration. Unlike most Extreme Programming teams, they must schedule their partner-swapping because they only have two pairs of developers.

- **On-site customer:** In this case the developers will be on-site at the customer's premises.

- **Small releases:** After each iteration the software will be released for customer testing and evaluation, but it will only go into production at the end of the project.

Inception

At Acme Inc. the accounting manager, Karen, has been under pressure to reduce costs, so she has proposed a new billing system to integrate the various financial applications used by the accounting team. The same data wouldn't have to be entered several times into different systems, and this would eliminate three full-time data-entry positions and save the company about $150,000 a year. Karen's boss, Salim, was keen on the idea, but he was also concerned about the cost of the new application. He wanted to keep it below $300,000 so that the project would have a two-year payback period.

Salim contacted People Co., who suggested that he hire an established team of four developers with a good mix of experience and skills. He also found an experienced project manager from within Acme's Operations department, Phil, who could devote at least half his time to managing the project.

When Salim asked Angela, the lead developer, to estimate the cost and duration of the project, she replied that "At this stage the requirements are still very imprecise. All I can say is that it'll probably take between one and 12 months to create this software. I suggest we first organize a two-week scoping study to firm up the requirements as much as possible before we plan the rest of the project. We can then decide how many more two-week iterations we'll need to complete the work."

Salim wanted to include Karen in the project team to define the requirements, but Angela disagreed. "Your data entry supervisor, Emily, knows much more about the accounting applications, and how the team uses them. Besides, we'll need this person on the team for the whole of the project, and I don't think that Karen can spare that much time. She would need to set aside at least 20 hours a week."

The project team was therefore organized as shown in Table 7-1.

Table 7-1. The Members of the Project Team

Resource	Name	Specialty	Hourly Rate	Effort per Iteration	Cost per Iteration
Lead developer	Angela	Architecture	$120.00	80 hours	$9,600
Senior developer	Govind	Networks	$85.00	80 hours	$6,800
Developer	Rauna	Databases	$75.00	80 hours	$6,000
Junior developer	Karl	User interfaces	$60.00	80 hours	$4,800
End user	Emily	Business issues	$50.00	40 hours	$2,000
Project manager	Phil	Client liaison	$100.00	40 hours	$4,000
TOTAL					$33,200

Scoping Study

The scoping study started off with a three-day requirements workshop in a conference room with a printing whiteboard. The focus was on mapping out exactly how the new application was going to work. The four developers sat around the table with Emily, and they helped her lay out the data fields and buttons for each of the new screens, and step through each of the use cases for the new system. They took turns writing up notes about the discussion.

On Thursday the developers gathered in the same room, this time without Emily, to create a high-level design for the system. As the expert on software architecture, Angela led the discussion, but she tried to include all of the developers in the discussion by asking them questions related to their areas of expertise. The architecture for the system was sketched on the whiteboard in a series of UML diagrams.

Govind and Rauna then worked together to develop a small piece of functionality that passed some data all the way from the front-end user interface to a back-end web service. They expected to complete this work within a week, but the actual pace they achieved and the problems they encountered would provide valuable information as to how fast the remaining work could be expected to progress.

Meanwhile, Angela and Karl concentrated on writing up the results of the week's discussions. Karl wrote up the use cases as a series of documents, and created mock-up screens for the new application with the team's software development tools. Angela spent the time writing up the architecture document. She used a UML drawing program for the diagrams, and added some text that explained why the architecture was the way it was. There was also discussion of the main technical risks, which Angela had spent some time researching and, wherever possible, resolving.

She also broke down Emily's requirements into a list of 73 individual features, and gave initial estimates for each of these features of between one and five units of work. Each unit initially represented a day's work for a developer, but this conversion factor could be adjusted if the overall pace was found to be faster or slower. This meant that the estimates for individual features wouldn't have to be changed if the pace varied. Features that came out as larger than five units were broken down still further.

Project Planning Meeting

On Friday the developers got back together with Emily and Phil to go over the requirements and the estimates. After Karl demonstrated the mock application, the developers asked Emily and Phil to divide up the feature list into must-do, should-do, and could-do features.

"They're all must-do features," said Emily, "We need all of these features in the application."

"We define must-do a little differently from that," replied Rauna. "A must-do feature is one where if it's not there, then the application is of absolutely no use to anyone, and there's no point in deploying it."

"What about should-do and could-do?" asked Phil.

"A should-do feature is one where you can quantify, or at least point to the feature's business value. It has to directly save you money. A could-do feature is one that has no business value of its own, but which helps you to use the features that do," said Rauna.

After some discussion, the team members were able to divide up the feature list as follows:

- Must-do: 29 features

- Should-do: 23 features

- Could-do: 21 features

- Total: 73 features

"Are you guys OK with the estimates I came up with?" asked Angela.

"I think the estimates for the web services need to be increased," replied Govind. "From the work we've been doing, it looks like we'll need to coordinate the database and web service updates with transactions. But web services don't support transactions yet, so we'll have to use a workaround where we create an 'undo' web service that is called whenever a transaction is aborted."

"How much is that going to increase the estimates by?" asked Angela.

"We'll have to create an undo web service for each functional web service, which will double the amount of work we have to do in that area," said Govind.

"OK. Is there anything else?" asked Angela.

"Well, some of the screens are wrong," said Emily, "I've marked the changes on these printouts. We'll have to add some fields and change the names of some others. Also, these two screens have to be combined into one."

"That doesn't look too major. Apart from reworking the bits that Govind and Rauna have already finished, we can probably do the rest in the same time as before," said Karl.

With these changes, the estimates came out as

- Must-do: 83 units

- Should-do: 56 units

- Could-do: 58 units

- Total: 197 units

"Over the last few projects, the team has averaged 20 units per week—or perhaps half that during the Elaboration phase—so we're looking at about ten weeks work here," said Angela. "Govind and Rauna completed features worth 11 units last week, so the estimated pace is about right for this project. We'll need an Elaboration iteration of about 20 units, and then maybe four Construction iterations of 40 units each. That adds up to 191 units. Can we trim a couple of features to reduce the scope by 6 units? Otherwise we'll need to allow for an extra iteration."

"I think that we can lose these two features. The users don't need to resize the data entry windows if they're sensibly laid out, and pop-up help is not essential if the users are properly trained," said Phil.

"I agree: they're not quite as important as the rest. I can go along with that, so long as we don't lose any more," said Emily.

"OK. That gives us a project plan that looks like this," said Angela as she passed around copies of Table 7-2 and Figure 7-1.

Table 7-2. The Duration, Scope, and Cost of the Project's Phases

Phase	Iterations	Duration	Units	Cost
Scoping Study	1	2 weeks	11	$33,200
Elaboration	1	2 weeks	20	$33,200
Construction	4	8 weeks	160	$132,800
Transition	1	2 weeks		$33,200
Contingency	2	4 weeks		$66,400
TOTAL	9	18 weeks	191	$298,800

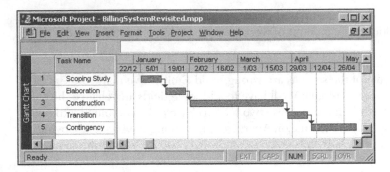

Figure 7-1. The overall project plan

"Why do we need so much contingency?" asked Phil.

"We actually need more than this. At the product definition stage, estimates are only accurate to a factor of 2, so we should allow at least 50 percent contingency. But if we can make all of the could-do features optional, then that gives us another 37 percent contingency. Combined with the two extra iterations, that's a total contingency of 68 percent, which should be more than enough," said Angela (see Figure 7-2).

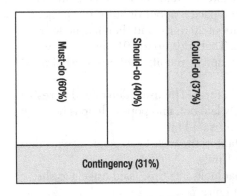

Figure 7-2. The shaded area represents the total contingency for the project. In addition to the time allocated to the essential must-do and could-do functionality, another 68 percent can be used for resolving problems.

"We still want you to include all of the could-do features," said Emily.

"Yes. That's why the contingency iterations are there. I'm confident that the estimates are within 30 percent of what they should be, so if there are any overruns, then we can still complete all the features with only one or two extra iterations. However, and I think this is very unlikely, if something does go badly wrong, then at least we'll be able to create software that still meets your most pressing needs," said Angela.

"I think I can get Salim to give us the go-ahead for that. The budget is very close to what he was looking for," said Phil.

"We'll see you on Monday then," said Angela.

Elaboration

The first task was to set up the team's office for pair programming (Figure 7-3). Instead of the usual corner desks, the team had requested straight worktables. They put two of these back to back, each with a workstation and two chairs for a pair of developers. The third table was placed end-on to these two, so Emily or Phil could work alongside the team whenever they needed to. The development team faced each other as they worked, which made their discussions easier.

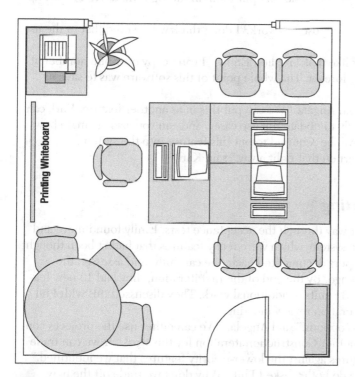

Figure 7-3. The layout of the team's office

After that, they set up the development environment for the project, including a source code repository and an automated build script. Govind and Rauna merged their work and Karl's mock-up screens into this structure. The existing unit tests were included in the build script. The team also decided on a process configuration for RUP, but this didn't take long as they could reuse one they'd already used successfully on several projects of about the same size and duration.

For this iteration, Karl decided to work with Govind, and Rauna with Angela. Between them, they divided up some of the highest-risk, must-do features so that each pair of developers was assigned ten units of work. This work included the undo web service for Govind and Rauna's already completed web service. The remaining time was allocated to analyzing the effects of the inevitable change requests on the requirements and the high-level design.

In the meantime, Emily began working on a set of acceptance tests for the system, based on the use cases that Karl had written up. The first one that she wrote was for the functionality that Govind and Rauna had already completed. When she tried it out, she found that it didn't work the way she expected it to.

She looked up from her screen and said, "Hey guys, this first screen doesn't work properly. I've just tried to copy some lines from a spreadsheet to paste them into this screen, but it doesn't put them in the right fields. It all ends up in the first field."

"Is that how it's supposed to work? I don't think we covered that in the use cases," said Karl.

"It has to work like that," replied Emily, "I can't copy over one number at a time. That'll take forever. The whole point of this software was to save us time."

"That's OK," said Angela. "We can put this in as another feature. Karl, can you work with Emily to update the use cases, and can you also estimate how much extra work will be required to put this feature into the system?"

"Sure. I can start on that right away," said Karl.

Review Meeting

As she worked her way through the acceptance tests, Emily found more and more "bugs" in the system, which were really features that hadn't been thought of yet. The developers documented each one carefully, and assessed the impact of each change. By the end of the first iteration, they had 13 new features that came to 34 units of additional work. They discussed this with Phil at the two-week iteration review meeting.

"We've got two options," said Angela, "We can either use the project's contingency to add another Construction iteration for this work, or we can trade off these new features against the lower-priority features that we identified."

"Why don't we do both?" asked Phil. "Why don't we trade off the new must-do and should-do features against the old could-do features, and then decide after the fourth Construction iteration whether we want to add a fifth iteration for the remaining could-do features? At that point we'll know whether we're running behind schedule, and whether we can afford to use up the contingency time."

"I can go along with that," replied Emily, "but only if you promise that we will do that extra iteration if we're not too far behind. We still need those features in the software."

"What was the progress for this iteration?" asked Phil.

"We finished 7 features that added up to 18 units," said Govind.

"That's a bit slow. We planned 20 units this iteration, didn't we?" asked Phil.

"Yes, but we'd expect some variation, because the estimate for each feature might be off by a few percent. We've done 29 units against a plan of 31 at this point, so I still think that our estimates are broadly correct," said Angela.

"Are there any other issues?" asked Phil.

"Well," said Govind, "I had some difficulties getting the default .NET web service interfaces to work with some of the accounting applications. They need their data formatted in a strange way. I could get it to work in the end, but I had to create the interfaces by hand."

"What does this mean for the project?" asked Phil.

"It'll take a bit longer to create the interfaces manually, but not too much. I suggest that we add two more units of work to the estimates. Also, I'm the only one who knows how to create these interfaces, so I'll have to pair with anyone who has to work on one of them. This might disrupt our pair programming rotation a bit," said Govind.

"We can work around that, though," said Angela.

Construction

The team continued to make steady progress (Table 7-3).

Table 7-3. Progress During the Project's Iterations

Iteration	Expected Progress (units)	Expected Total (units)	Actual Progress (units)	Actual Total (units)
Scoping study	11	11	11	11
Elaboration	20	31	18	29
Construction 1	40	71	35	64
Construction 2	40	111	32	96
Construction 3	40	151	43	139
Construction 4	40	191	33	172
Construction 5			37	209

Phil was concerned when the team slipped behind schedule by 5 units in the first Construction iteration, and he became even more worried when he saw this trend increasing in the next iteration. He scheduled a private meeting with Angela to discuss the issue.

"What's the problem, Angela? Why aren't you meeting your targets?"

"To be honest, Phil, I'm not sure," she replied, "The guys haven't encountered any significant problems so far. It's possible that the estimates were just a little on the low side. Also, the earlier features required more of the infrastructure to be created, whereas we defined the features from a user perspective, so that may be why this work is taking longer than expected."

"How are you planning to make up the time?"

"Phil, the figures we gave you were estimates—not targets," she said, "A realistic estimate is just as likely to be too small as it is to be too big. We made a commitment to develop this software in the most efficient way possible, and we assured you that the development wouldn't overrun its contingency. And it won't. At this rate we'll still be well within our overall budget."

"So what do you suggest we do?"

"We still have to see, but I think we're going to need that fifth iteration after all."

With each iteration, the software that Emily was testing became more and more complete. Whenever she got a new version, she ran through her acceptance tests to confirm that all of the new features worked as expected. She also spent time playing with the new system, trying a variety of tasks in different ways, and by doing so she uncovered a few small but significant bugs.

As before, most of the bugs she reported were actually changes to the requirements, but the major ones had already been identified and superficial changes could be accommodated within the existing estimates. The developers worked closely with Emily to ensure that each new feature that they tackled worked exactly the way she wanted it to.

Construction Iteration 5

At the close-out meeting for the fourth Construction iteration, the team had to decide whether to go ahead with a fifth iteration.

"How are we doing overall?" asked Phil.

"We've finished 66 features out of 72, and there are 6 features remaining, which come to 19 units in total," said Angela. "There are also a few outstanding bugs that Emily found, but most of them are quite minor. The formatting on some of the screens and reports can get stuffed up if the data items are too long, but that should only take a few hours to fix. Apart from that, the software passes all of our unit tests, and all of Emily's acceptance tests."

"It sounds like both the software and the project are in good shape. I think we can use up some of that contingency time. We had 36 units of could-do features that were traded off in the Elaboration phase. Do you think you can finish half of those, plus the remaining features, in one more iteration?" asked Phil.

"I'm confident that we can do at least some of them," replied Angela. "Let's plan to do 32 units in this iteration—that seems safe in view of the pace so far—and then we'll see what else we can get done. Emily, you'll have to update the acceptance tests to include these new features. If we could have them by the end of next week, then that'll give us enough time to ensure that everything is working properly before the end of the iteration."

The *burn-down chart* displayed on the office wall was extended to show the new iteration and the additional scope (Figure 7-4).

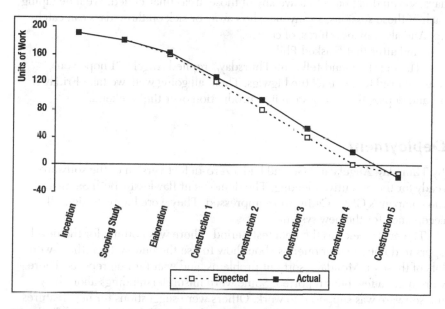

Figure 7-4. The pace of work during the project

The developers were able to complete 37 units of work during those two weeks, so during the second week they asked Emily which additional features she would most like to see implemented. She picked out 2 more features that were worth 5 units together.

At the close-out meeting for the fifth Construction iteration, Emily argued strongly for a sixth iteration to complete all of the remaining features. "These were requirements that we said we needed right at the beginning of this project. We still have time on hand. Why don't we just do them too? And there are a few more things that I've come up with that we should include too."

Phil disagreed. "I'm sorry, but I'd rather keep some time in hand in case there are any problems during the Transition phase. What happens if the beta test goes badly, and we need to fix a whole lot more bugs? No. We decided that these features were the least important ones, and I don't think we'll miss much if they're not included in the final version of the system."

Transition

"So what's the plan for the Transition phase?" asked Phil.

"Angela and Govind will spend the next few days closing out the remaining defects and putting everything in order," said Rauna. "Karl and I will be in charge of training. We'd like to train your help desk on Monday, the system administrators on Tuesday, and the data entry operators on Wednesday. We're planning to do a morning session and an afternoon session on each of these days, so you don't have to leave any of those areas unattended. We'll be taping each of these sessions, so anyone who's away or sick on those days can catch up. And also any new hires, of course."

"And after that?" asked Phil.

"The big show-and-tell is on Thursday," replied Angela. "I hope you remembered to invite all the bigwigs. Then, all going well, we take Friday off and deploy the new system into production over the weekend."

Deployment

By Thursday, Angela and Govind had a zero-defect version of the software ready for the executive meeting. The demo went flawlessly. Both Salim and the company's CEO, Cathy, were impressed. They were happy to sign off acceptance for the new system.

The next week was the beta test period. There was nothing for the developers to do but answer queries about how to use the new system (there were lots of these on Monday), sort out problems, and wait for bug reports. There were quite a few bugs reported. Some were misunderstandings about how the software was supposed to work. Others were suggestions for new features and changes that were carefully documented; a few of these deserved further investigation. They eventually ended up with just two new bugs that needed fixing, and Govind and Karl volunteered to work on these.

Angela and Rauna took the Wednesday off, as they had to come back the following weekend to install the final version of the software. On Friday there was a project close-out meeting where the outstanding issues were aired— these were mainly suggestions for new features—and the project was declared a success. Phil opened a bottle of champagne to celebrate, and afterwards the developers went back to clean out their office.

Aftermath

After the project, Phil went over the financials one last time. The project had gone very smoothly, and only half the planned project management time had been used, which saved about $16,000. The project had come in early by two weeks, and that saved a further $33,200. The overall cost of the project was just over $250,000 (Figure 7-5), and the payback period was now just 20 months.

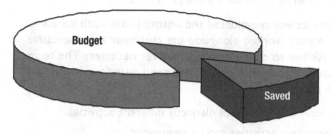

Figure 7-5. The savings from the original budget

The users were mostly happy with the new system, although there was a growing list of suggestions for additional features. Salim didn't see these as high priority, though, because most of them offered no direct financial benefit.

Cathy was very pleased with the results of the project. "I think that there may be a bonus in this for you guys," she said to Salim and Phil.

Summary

Why did this case study succeed when the previous one in Chapter 4 failed? If we compare this case study to the list of invalid assumptions identified in Chapter 3, we can see that the techniques used by the team helped them to avoid these assumptions, and thereby achieve a better result:

1. Scope can be completely defined.
2. Scope definition can be done before the project starts.

The scope of the project was reevaluated and adjusted after each iteration. Moreover, the developers worked alongside the customer representative (Emily), and could ask her to clarify details whenever necessary. The team used triage and feature trade-off to ensure that total quantity of work did not overwhelm the budget.

3. Software development consists of distinctly different activities.
4. Software development activities can be sequenced.
5. Team members can be individually allocated to activities.

The team's development process combined design, construction, and testing, so the design could be refined as required and the software could be tested from day one. The developers collaborated on gathering requirements, defining the architecture, and producing estimates, so everyone had an opportunity to ask questions and make suggestions. Communication was abundant and effective.

6. The size of the project team does not affect the development process.

The team was very small, and the developers were able to adopt a very informal and efficient development process. They used a Rational Unified Process configuration that had been customized for the size of the team, and adapted the Extreme Programming practices for their circumstances

7. There is always a way to produce meaningful estimates.
8. Acceptably accurate estimates can be obtained.
9. One developer is equivalent to another.

Using a SWAT team allowed the estimates to be based on the results of the team's previous projects, making them more accurate. The amount of contingency reserve—partly based on triage—was more than adequate for the degree of inaccuracy in the estimates. The scoping study also gave the developers an opportunity to check their expected level of productivity against the project's specific circumstances.

10. Metrics are sufficient to assess the quality of software.

The developers continually assessed the quality of each other's code during pair programming. Automated unit testing helped the developers become aware of new bugs very rapidly, so the software maintained a low level of defects. Ongoing acceptance testing by the end user ensured that the usability and functionality of the software were also assessed.

8

Afterword

A software project can fail even before it starts. It can fail just because of the way it has been organized and set up. Often it's impossible to find out whether a project has failed until just before it's due to end. Only when the software is ready for testing and deployment does its poor quality become apparent.

The advantage of iterative development is that each iteration provides another chance to find out what's going wrong, and another chance to put it right. However, to do iterative development properly, you must make dramatic changes to the way you manage your projects. Many project management best practices just won't work anymore.

Software is strange stuff: it's complex, abstract, and fluid. It helps to have a deep understanding of the peculiar nature of software when you're planning a software development project. Nontechnical people—customers and project managers—often haven't had the kind of hands-on experience that's needed to achieve this level of understanding. However, the technical members of the team—the developers, architects, and analysts—often lack the business and management skills needed to successfully organize a project.

The conceptual gap between the technical and nontechnical members of a software development team is the most obvious reason why software projects fail. The communication of requirements from customers to developers is a common source of problems, as is the communication from developers to customers of the repercussions of those requirements.

Developers often concentrate on technology to the exclusion of everything else, and they invariably propose technical solutions to nontechnical problems. They need a detailed understanding of the business issues that the software is intended to address, and they should be asked to think about what they can do to help the project run more smoothly.

Developers can also bring essential input to the project planning process. All too often, developers are brought onto the team only when the project has been completely planned. Developers are the experts in software development. If their input has been ignored, then how realistic will the plan be?

The key to software development success is frequent, ongoing communication between the developers, the customer, and the project manager throughout the project, with regular opportunities to confirm understanding and give feedback. By making use of the techniques discussed in this book, you can improve your team's communication, and ensure that your software projects succeed.

Appendix:
The Agile Manifesto

In early 2001 a small group of methodology thought leaders gathered in a ski resort in Utah to find out whether there was any common ground between their seemingly disparate methodologies: Extreme Programming, SCRUM, DSDM, Adaptive Software Development, Crystal, Feature-Driven Development, and others. After two days of vigorous debate, they agreed that the term "agile" best described their new kind of methodology. They were also able to agree on a number of common goals, outlined in the following manifesto.

Manifesto for Agile Software Development

We are uncovering better ways of developing software by doing it and helping others do it. Through this work we have come to value:

- **Individuals and interactions** over processes and tools
- **Working software** over comprehensive documentation
- **Customer collaboration** over contract negotiation
- **Responding to change** over following a plan

That is, while there is value in the items on the right, we value the items on the left more.

Kent Beck, Mike Beedle, Arie van Bennekum, Alistair Cockburn,
Ward Cunningham, Martin Fowler, James Grenning, Jim Highsmith,
Andrew Hunt, Ron Jeffries, Jon Kern, Brian Marick, Robert C. Martin,
Steve Mellor, Ken Schwaber, Jeff Sutherland, Dave Thomas.

© 2001, the above authors

This declaration may be freely copied in any form, but only in its entirety through this notice.

Glossary

acceptance tests   These are a set of structured **system tests** that have been defined by the customer, and are often based on the **use cases** in the system requirements. Software development contracts often state that the software must pass acceptance testing before it can be delivered and the final payment made.

application   A piece of software that can run on its own, but which often connects to other systems. It's also known as a computer program. There are the one-person desktop applications that we're all familiar with, such as Microsoft Word for word processing, but there are also multiuser applications that run on an office network, such as accounting and email. Beyond that are applications we use over the Internet, such as Amazon.com's online ordering and Google's search page, and applications that other applications use to exchange information, so that international phone calls can get connected, for example.

architecture   The internal design of a piece of software, taken at a high level, that allows the software to fulfill its requirements. It shows how the constituent **components** make up the software, and how it connects to external systems such as a **database** or another **application**.

artifact   The product of an activity during software development. Examples of artifacts include a **project** plan, an **architecture** document, a set of **unit tests**, an **acceptance test** plan, some **components**, an entire **application**, a user manual, and so on.

best practice   A process or technique that has a proven record of success in providing significant improvement to the results of an activity such as software development or project management.

beta testing   Testing software by releasing it to a small group of carefully chosen customers for them to use in real-world conditions. These tests aren't structured in any way. Customers often use software in ways that developers can't predict, so this form of testing finds **bugs** and usability problems that are missed by **unit testing** and **system testing**.

bug   A defect or error in the software that makes it behave in a way that it's not supposed to.

build process   An **application** that has been configured to automatically perform all of the steps required to **integrate** a piece of software and create its **executable**. It can also perform the **unit tests** for the software, to check that everything still works properly. The build process can be scheduled to run on a regular basis: either every hour, every night, or over the weekend, depending on how long the process takes to complete.

burn-down chart   A diagram that demonstrates progress by showing how the quantity of work remaining to be done has decreased over the course of the **project** [Cockburn 2004].

business logic   The business processes and rules that are implemented in an **application**. For example, an insurance company might define a formula that calculates the premium for a driver from their driving history and the value of their car.

class   An **object** is created in a program according to the definition provided by its class.

code   Short for **source code**.

compile, to   To convert **source code** into an **executable**.

component   A piece of software that can't run on its own, but must be incorporated into or used by an **application**. A component is something that can be deployed as a black box: it hides the complexity of its internal mechanisms behind a simple interface. It contains data as well as **routines** that operate on that data. A component works in the same way as an **object**, but on a larger scale. A component can contain many **objects**.

Components can be purchased from third-party vendors, or they can be created by developers to reduce the level of complexity in their software.

database   A collection of data that's organized in a structured way. A company's databases are kept on a **server**, and are accessed via database software such as Oracle Database or Microsoft SQL Server.

encapsulation   A technique to reduce the overall level of complexity in a piece of software by isolating various parts of the system from each other. These are sectioned off into **objects** or **components**. It is a key part of **object-oriented programming**.

enterprise application framework Nowadays any significant new software is almost certain to be built with an enterprise **application** framework such as Sun Microsystems' Java 2 Enterprise Edition (J2EE) or Microsoft .NET. A framework is a toolkit, just like a Lego set, that you can use to build a variety of items. In the case of software, the building blocks are bits of software which do jobs that have been found useful in a wide range of situations. Examples include getting data from a **database**, drawing a window on the screen, or converting dates from one format to another.

"Enterprise" is a difficult word to define. Perhaps the best way to think of it is "as big as you want." Desktop **applications** are limited to running on one computer, but that's OK because only one person is using them at a time. The popular Internet search engine Google provides information to more than 1,000 people every second: no single computer could handle that load. Enterprise technology allows many computers to work together for a single **application**, and also provides the connectivity to allow lots of people to access it at the same time. But "enterprise" also means "as small as you want": enterprise application frameworks are not just for major **applications** in big companies.

executable The set of **instructions** or operations that makes up a piece of software, but written in a format that only the computer can understand. An executable can't normally be converted back into a form that a person can understand.

extensibility The ability to extend or modify a piece of software without damaging the way that it works. Extensibility isn't apparent when the software is first completed; it only shows up when you try to make changes to the software.

feature An intended property or behavior of a piece of software. For example, Microsoft Word's ability to emphasize misspelled words is a feature of the program.

fragile code **Source code** that may work well, but in which it's virtually impossible to make changes without introducing new **bugs**, and breaking some of its existing functionality. Code becomes fragile when its **architecture** doesn't receive enough attention and expertise.

functional specification A document that describes in great detail the **features** and functions of a piece of software. It defines the requirements and **scope** for the **project** that creates the software.

instruction This is usually a single line of **source code**, but very complex instructions sometimes span two or more lines. An instruction may copy a piece of data, perform some arithmetic, manipulate text, invoke a **routine** in an internal or external **component**, or decide which parts of the program to execute (and in what order).

integration   The process of building the **executable** for an **application** or **component** by **compiling** the **source code** to a format the computer can understand, and then incorporating or connecting to other **components**.

iteration   An iteration is a small part of a project that contains all of the steps required to design and build a portion of the software. It starts with choosing a set of **features** to be added. The overall **architecture** for the software is then extended and adjusted to accommodate the new **features**. Once these **features** have been developed and tested, the developers can put together and evaluate an updated version of the software.

legacy software   An **application** or system that is already in production. It may rely on old versions of technologies, or even technologies that are totally obsolete.

method   A **routine** that's defined in a **class**, and is available in an **object**.

methodology   A set of procedures and guidelines for some or all of the software development process. A methodology may contain step-by-step descriptions to show how to perform individual activities, flowcharts to show how activities are interrelated, and **metrics** to evaluate whether the activities were completed successfully.

metric   This defines, in very specific terms, what something is and how it's measured. For example, the number of new **bugs** found and the number of existing **bugs** resolved during an **iteration** are two useful metrics that can help a team to assess its progress.

object   A piece of software that can't run on its own, but must be incorporated into or used by an **application**. An object is something that can be used as a black box: it hides the complexity of its internal mechanisms behind a simple interface. It contains data as well as **routines** that operate on that data. An object works in the same way as a **component**, but on a smaller scale. A **component** can contain many objects. Objects are rarely downloaded or purchased individually.

object-oriented programming   A set of techniques and **architectural** patterns that are used when building software out of **objects**.

open source   When you buy or download software, you normally receive only the **executable**—not the **source code**. Open source software includes **source code** alongside the **executable**, so that anyone who wants to can find out how the software works, and make changes to fix **bugs** and add the **features** they want. The Linux operating system kernel is a well-known example of open source software.

outsourcing   Sending out software development work to another company, which the customer might otherwise give to their own staff. Outsourcing is usually done to cut costs, by allowing companies to specialize, but it also allows a company to rapidly increase or decrease the pace of development without having to hire or fire staff.

payback period This **metric** represents the payback time for an investment. To achieve a two-year payback period, for example, a new piece of software must enhance revenue or save costs equivalent to its development budget during the first two years in production.

process In contrast to a **project**, a process is a sequence of activities, people, and systems involved in creating a product or service in a repeatable way.

project In contrast to a **process**, a project is a temporary endeavor undertaken to create a unique product or service. A project may include **processes** for the parts of the project that are repeatable.

quality assurance A system of standards and procedures, such as sampling, that ensures that an acceptable level of quality is maintained.

refactor, to To restructure existing **code** without changing its functionality in any way. The aim is to clean up and simplify the design so that further progress can be made as rapidly as possible. The risk of introducing new **bugs** will have been minimized. As the developers write the **code**, they learn what is needed in its design, and they continually revise the overall **architecture**.

risk An uncertain event or condition that has consequences for the **project** or **process**; for example, that an essential third-party software component isn't available in time.

role A specialization that someone might assume during a software development project: for example, architect, business analyst, programmer, or tester. Each role is given responsibility for a number of activities, and each role has one or more individuals assigned to it, who might have specific experience that suits them particularly to that role. People often take on more than one role, particularly in small teams.

routine The set of **instructions** contained in a small chunk of **source code**, which perform a single, well-defined task, and are grouped together for convenience, for example, converting dates from one format to another.

scope A clear and complete definition of the overall aims of a project. It's normally broken down into a number of smaller, more closely defined goals.

server A computer that doesn't have a user sitting in front of it. A server can run a shared **application**, accommodate a **database**, or host some shared **components**, perhaps as **web services**. The word "server" is sometimes used to refer to a server **application** such as BizTalk Server or SQL Server, but this usage is incorrect.

source code The set of **instructions** that makes up a piece of software, but written in a format that a person can understand. Before the software can be run on a computer, it must be **compiled** into an **executable** so the computer can understand it.

system test   Unlike a **unit test**, a system test tries out some **features** on the software as a whole. System tests imitate what a user would do with the software, but it's very hard to create system tests for every situation or error that could possibly occur.

technical specification   A document that describes in great detail how a piece of software should work. It normally includes both a high-level **architecture** and detailed design work.

test engine   Software that allows you to configure and run **unit tests** or **system tests** by defining the expected output for some input data.

UML   The Unified Modeling Language is a visual modeling language from the Object Management Group. It allows you to create a "map" for software that shows its structure in greater or lesser detail. By hiding details, you can create a comprehensible overview of the system, and by exposing details you can show exactly how a small part of it works.

Visual models are used to depict the **architecture** and design of the software, and to communicate these to the development team. The quality of the **architecture** is easier to see in visual models, and by maintaining a good **architecture**, the quality of the resulting software will be improved. As the software is modified, various tools can be used to keep visual models and code synchronized with each other.

unit test   Unlike a **system test**, a unit test takes only a small part of the software and tests its functionality in isolation from the rest of the system. It's time consuming but relatively easy to create unit tests for every situation or error that could possibly occur.

use case   A technique for communicating requirements in a simple, but structured and unambiguous way with customers who may have no technical expertise whatsoever. A use case defines a sequence of actions that ends up with a result that's of some value to whoever performs them. Defining the requirements in this way gives the developers enough detail to work with, but the fact that the use case's result has value also makes it meaningful to the customer.

Use cases are a convenient way to group individual **features**. The collection of use cases defines the complete set of **features** that the system will have. Subsets of this group can be used to define the scope of individual **iterations**. The use case descriptions make it easy to do **system testing**: you simply perform each step in every use case. The use cases can also be converted into step-by-step user documentation.

user interface   The windows, menus, buttons, and fields in a software **application** that display data and respond to the user's actions. This is the part of the program that the user sees, and they often have firm ideas on how it should look.

web service   For all the hype surrounding web services, they are in principle very simple. Instead of selling CD-ROMs, a vendor keeps their software **components** on their own **servers** and makes them available over the Internet for a fee. This makes it easy for the vendor to apply **bug** fixes and enhancements, and enables them to provide access to interesting data (stock quotes, news, retail price comparisons, etc.) as well as useful tools.

workaround   A temporary procedure or approach used to bypass or avoid a **bug** or limitation in a system. A developer can write extra **code** as a workaround for the limitations of some tool or **component**. A user can perform additional steps when they use an **application**, as a workaround for its **bugs**.

Further Reading

Anderson, David. *Agile Management for Software Engineering: Applying the Theory of Constraints for Business Results.* Prentice Hall PTR, 2004.

Anderson applies a new accounting technique to measuring the value of software development work. The aim is to achieve business goals more efficiently. He shows how the theory can be applied to agile methodologies such as Scrum, Extreme Programming, and Feature-Driven Development.

Anthes, Gary. *ROI Guide: Payback Period.* Computerworld, 17 February 2003. http://www.computerworld.com/managementtopics/roi/story/0,10801,78529,00.html.

A clear explanation of the term "payback period."

Auer, Ken and Roy Miller. *Extreme Programming Applied: Playing to Win.* Addison-Wesley, 2002.

One of a raft of very similar books that have been published about XP. This one focuses on getting started with the various techniques, and is a good introduction.

Bell, Stephen. *Justice ministry begins fixing error-ridden Courts system.* Computerworld, 27 April 2004. http://www.computerworld.co.nz/news.nsf/UNID/7256ECB173FBC19DCC256E81007D3CAF.

A postmortem of a typical software project that "showed many of the classic shortcomings identified in delayed, over-budget and abandoned projects."

Boehm, Barry. *Software Engineering Economics.* Prentice Hall PTR, 1981.

An overview of microeconomics as applied to software development. A classic in its time, this book is now starting to show its age. Still well worth reading, though.

Brooks, Frederick. *The Mythical Man-Month: Essays on Software Engineering, 20th Anniversary Edition.* Addison-Wesley, 1995.

The classic book on the human elements of software engineering.

Cade, Mark and Simon Roberts. *Sun Certified Enterprise Architect for J2EE Technology Study Guide.* Prentice Hall PTR, 2002.

A handy overview of enterprise-level software architecture concepts, particularly for J2EE.

Cockburn, Alistair. *Characterizing People as Non-Linear, First-Order Components in Software Development.* Humans and Technology, 1999. http://alistair.cockburn.us/crystal/articles/cpanfocisd/characterizingpeopleasnonlinear.html.

Alistair Cockburn has had a number of brilliant insights into the way people actually develop software. This paper is a great introduction into some of those ideas.

———. *Agile Software Development.* Addison-Wesley, 2002.

A survey of the concepts and techniques behind agile software development. Useful tools to build your own methodology. More information is available at http://alistair.cockburn.us.

———. *Crystal Clear: A Human-Powered Methodology for Small Teams.* Addison-Wesley, 2004.

This book is the best description of a workable small-team methodology that I've yet seen. I've been working from an unpublished draft, and I can't wait to see it in print.

——— and Laurie Williams. *The Costs and Benefits of Pair Programming.* Humans and Technology, 2000. http://alistair.cockburn.us/crystal/articles/ppcb/pairprogrammingcostbene.html.

Research that proves the value of pair programming: use it to convince the skeptics in your organization.

Cooney, Matthew. *Agile processes keep customers happy.* ComputerWeekly, 13 May 2004. http://www.computerweekly.com/Article130531.htm.

Yes, agile development techniques do work. This article summarizes recent research on the successful adoption of agile methodologies, and includes an overview of XP, DSDM, and RUP.

Firesmith, Donald and Brian Henderson-Sellers. *The OPEN Process Framework: An Introduction.* Addison-Wesley, 2001.

This looks like a methodology designed by a committee. It aims to be all things to all people, but ends up being of little value to anyone. Not recommended.

Fowler, Martin. *The New Methodology.* ThoughtWorks, 2003. http://www.martinfowler.com/articles/newMethodology.html.

An excellent introduction to the agile movement, this article includes a broad survey of the existing agile methodologies.

———. *Using an Agile Software Process with Offshore Development.* ThoughtWorks, 2004. http://www.martinfowler.com/articles/agileOffshore.html.

Martin Fowler has made offshore development work in an agile way, and in this article he describes his approach and his experiences.

Gamma, Erich, Richard Helm, Ralph Johnson, and John Vlissides. *Design Patterns.* Addison-Wesley, 1995.

This is the seminal book that revolutionized object-oriented programming. It uses a formal approach to explain an abstract subject, and many people regard it as a difficult book. The fact that the examples are either in C++ or Smalltalk—which are both obsolete programming languages—doesn't help. It's worth the effort, though.

Gilb, Tom. *Principles of Software Engineering Management.* Addison-Wesley, 1989.

Tom Gilb's classic book describes the principles behind Evolutionary Project Management (also known as EPM or Evo), which was an early agile methodology that became quite influential even though its uptake was limited.

Gleik, James. *Chasing Bugs in the Electronic Village.* New York Times Magazine, 4 August 1992. http://www.around.com/bugs.html.

In January 1990 James Gleik bought one of the first copies of Microsoft's Word for Windows. What he didn't know was that he had just become an unwilling beta tester for a very buggy piece of software. A frustrating—and funny—saga ensues.

Hayes, Frank. *Big IT: Doomed.* Computerworld, 7 June 2004. http://www.computerworld.com/managementtopics/management/project/story/0,10801,93641,00.html.

A perfect case study of how agile development techniques helped a huge software project to succeed, after another huge project failed to accomplish the same task.

Highsmith, Jim. *Adaptive Software Development: A Collaborative Approach to Managing Complex Systems.* Dorset House Publishing Company, 1999.

A seminal agile methodology from one of the most active thought leaders in the field. It has a sound theoretical basis, but doesn't include as extensive a range of best practices as some of the newer methodologies. More information is available at http://www.adaptivesd.com.

———. *Agile Project Management: Creating Innovative Products.* Addison-Wesley, 2004.

Highsmith addresses many of the same issues as *Software Project Secrets*, but instead of adapting existing project management standards, he creates an innovative five-phase project management methodology. It is applicable to more than just software development, even though it uses many ideas from the agile methodologies.

Jacobson, Ivar, Grady Booch, and James Rumbaugh. *The Unified Software Development Process.* Addison-Wesley, 1999.

The original book about the Unified Process, this covers the subject in exhaustive detail. The material is important, but the presentation is dry and overly academic. Try Kruchten's [2000] book first.

Jones, Caspers. *Patterns of large software systems: Failure and success. Computer,* vol. 28, no. 3, March 1995.

An oft-cited study that shows the extent to which requirements arrive after development begins.

Koskinen, Jussi. *Software Maintenance Costs.* Information Technology Research Institute, University of Jyväskylä, 2004. http://www.cs.jyu.fi/~koskinen/smcosts.htm.

A useful overview of the research on this subject.

Kruchten, Philippe. *The Rational Unified Process, An Introduction, Second Edition.* Addison-Wesley, 2000.

It can be a little dry at times, but this book does present a concise and well-organized overview of RUP.

———. *Agility with RUP. Cutter IT Journal*, vol. 14, no. 12, December 2001.

This article addresses many of the criticisms that have been leveled at RUP by showing how RUP can be used in an agile way. There's a lot of promotion here, but also some valuable guidance on how to adapt RUP for specific projects.

Larman, Craig. *Applying UML and Patterns: An Introduction to Object-Oriented Analysis and Design and the Unified Process, Second Edition*. Prentice Hall PTR, 2002.

More than just an introductory guide to object-oriented programming, this book explains how to use RUP in an agile, effective and sensible way. Read this before, or instead of, *Design Patterns* [Gamma et al. 1995].

———. *Agile and Iterative Development: A Manager's Guide*. Addison-Wesley, 2004.

Larman tries to convince managers to use agile methodologies in their software development projects by citing statistically significant research and a variety of case studies. He describes and compares Scrum, Extreme Programming, the Unified Process, and Evo in more detail than *Software Project Secrets*. This is the most compelling argument yet for agile development. Buy a copy for your manager.

———, Philippe Kruchten, and Kurt Bittner. *How to Fail with the Rational Unified Process: Seven Steps to Pain and Suffering*. Valtech Technologies & Rational Software, 2001. http://www.agilealliance.com/articles/reviews/Larman1/articles/How_to_Fail_with_the_RUP_-_Kruchten_and_Larman.pdf.

A humorous but effective essay that highlights the classic mistakes that people make in applying RUP, and shows how to avoid them.

McBreen, Pete. *Pretending to Be Agile*. informIT, 15 March 2002. http://www.informit.com/articles/article.asp?p=25913.

A succinct and pertinent description of what agile development really means.

McConnell, Steve. *Code Complete, Second Edition*. Microsoft Press, 2004.

Every developer should read this book, and their managers should at least skim it. It's a comprehensive guide to the techniques you need to make your code robust, readable, and error-free. There's extensive discussion about the issues behind the practices, and about software development in general.

———. *Rapid Development*. Microsoft Press, 1996.

A fantastic smorgasbord of ways to make your software project run more smoothly. Steve McConnell does his research, writes very readably, and takes the time to explain the background to the issues.

Microsoft. *Microsoft Solutions Framework Version 3.0 Overview White Paper*. Microsoft, 2003.

MSF is an alternative to the PMBOK that's specifically designed for software development. I like the approach, and particularly the way that project management responsibilities are shared around the team. More information is available at http://www.microsoft.com/msf.

Miller, Roy. *Managing Software for Growth: Without Fear, Control, and the Manufacturing Mindset.* Addison-Wesley, 2003. http://www.awprofessional.com/content/images/0321117433/samplechapter/millerch01.pdf.

Miller attributes software development failure to the "manufacturing mindset." His argument is a little different from mine, but it reaches much the same conclusions. It's interesting to compare this work to the Poppendiecks' [2003].

Palmer, Stephen and John Felsing. *A Practical Guide to Feature-Driven Development.* Prentice Hall PTR, 2002.

This methodology takes the middle ground between lightweight processes like XP and heavyweight processes like RUP. It's best for mid-range projects, but the concept itself is powerful, and can be useful in the context of any agile project. More information is available at http://www.featuredrivendevelopment.com.

Poppendieck, Mary and Tom. *Lean Software Development: An Agile Toolkit for Software Development Managers.* Addison-Wesley, 2003.

An intriguing new agile methodology that's based on the classic Lean Production principles from Toyota—also known as Just-In-Time manufacturing—which have revolutionized the industry. More information is available at http://www.poppendieck.com.

PMI—*see* Project Management Institute.

Project Management Institute. *A Guide to the Project Management Body of Knowledge (PMBOK Guide) – 2000 Edition.* Project Management Institute, 2000.

A surprisingly readable guide to the discipline, although it's clearly intended as a reference work. Beginners should consult an introductory workbook instead. More information is available at http://www.pmi.org.

——. *A Guide to the Project Management Body of Knowledge (PMBOK), Third Edition (2004), Exposure Draft.* Project Management Institute, 2004.

More text and diagrams than the previous edition; I found this one to be clearer and less dogmatic. Sadly, this is no longer available for free download.

Raymond, Eric. *The Cathedral and the Bazaar.* Thyrsus Enterprises, 2000a. http://www.catb.org/~esr/writings/cathedral-bazaar/cathedral-bazaar/.

This isn't just the story of Raymond's Fetchmail project, but also a profound philosophical exploration of open source development, how it works, and why people do it. Don't be put off by the level of technical detail.

——. *The Magic Cauldron.* Thyrsus Enterprises, 2000b. http://www.catb.org/~esr/writings/cathedral-bazaar/magic-cauldron/.

An intriguing analysis of the economics of software development. Raymond argues that there's much to be gained from sharing development expertise and costs by making many kinds of software open source.

Read, Robert. *How to Be a Programmer: A Short, Comprehensive, and Personal Survey.* Samizdat Press, 2003. http://samizdat.mines.edu/howto/.

A short and snappy guide to the social, personal, and general technical skills that are required to program well. A great introduction to the world of software development.

Redmill, Felix. *Software Projects: Evolutionary vs. Big-Bang Delivery.* John Wiley & Sons, 1997.

Redmill wrote about agile concepts before the term "agile" was even coined. This book didn't have a big impact at the time, but it pioneered many of the ideas that have subsequently been popularized by the agile methodologies. Interestingly, it presents these ideas in the context of software project management.

Royce, Walker. *Software Project Management: A Unified Framework.* Addison-Wesley, 1998.

Royce has created a new project management methodology for software development by extending the Unified Process. His book includes some sensible ideas, but it is beginning to seem a little dated.

Schwaber, Ken. *Agile Project Management with Scrum.* Microsoft Press, 2004.

This book explains how to apply Scrum's principles to software project management. It consists of case studies that are based on Schwaber's experience of helping teams implement Scrum.

—— and Mike Beedle. *Agile Software Development with SCRUM.* Prentice Hall, 2001.

A short and readable book that describes a simple and highly effective software development process. It focuses more on management than some of the other methodologies. It's increasingly widely used, and is gaining quite a reputation. More information is available at http://www.controlchaos.com.

Standish Group, The. *Extreme CHAOS.* The Standish Group, 2001. http://www.standishgroup.com/sample_research/PDFpages/extreme_chaos.pdf.

An update to the famous 1994 report that's universally referenced to show just how bad the situation is in software development.

Stapleton, Jennifer and DSDM Consortium. *DSDM: Business Focused Development, Second Edition.* Addison-Wesley, 2003.

The DSDM Consortium includes numerous British companies, universities, and government departments, and offers extensive resources, training, and certification. Unlike most of the other methodologies, this is not just a one-man band. More information is available at http://www.dsdm.org.

Thomsett, Rob. *Radical Project Management.* Prentice Hall PTR, 2002.

This book describes Extreme Project Management (XPM) as "the first radically new approach to project management in decades, designed from the ground up for today's high-speed, fast-changing projects." Thomsett draws a firm distinction between project management and "technical management"—the software development methodology—but he fails to explain how the two should work together.

Williams, Sam. *When offshoring goes bad.* Salon.com, 6 April 2004. http://www.salon.com/tech/feature/2004/04/06/offshoring_bad/index.html.

Offshore outsourcing isn't risk free, and there can be a real downside. This article deftly analyzes the risks, rewards, and potential of an increasingly popular trend.

Wysocki, Robert and Rudd McGary. *Effective Project Management: Traditional, Adaptive, Extreme, Third Edition.* Wiley Publishing, 2003.

This is a good, general introduction to the subject.

Yager, Tom. *BizTalk Server brings everybody into the process.* InfoWorld, 23 April 2004.
http://www.infoworld.com/article/04/04/23/17TCbiztalk_1.html.

A general overview of BizTalk Server 2004.

Yourdon, Edward. *Death March, Second Edition.* Prentice Hall PTR, 2004a.

This book tells you what to do when good projects go bad, or bad projects get worse. Readable and valuable, it might just save your sanity and your career. A classic.

———. *Outsource: Competing in the Global Productivity Race.* Prentice Hall PTR, 2004b.

A sequel to the prophetic *Decline and Fall of the American Programmer*, this book analyzes the recent interest in the offshore outsourcing of software development.

Index